CW00373525

Armada 1588

Armada 1588
The Spanish Assault
on England

John Barratt

Campaign Chronicle
Series Editor

Christopher Summerville

Pen & Sword
MILITARY

First published in Great Britain in 2005 by
Pen & Sword Military
an imprint of
Pen & Sword Books Ltd
47 Church Street
Barnsley
South Yorkshire
S70 2AS

ISBN 1-84415-323-1

A CIP catalogue record for this book is available from the British Library

Typeset in Garamond 11/13.5 pt by
Palindrome

Printed and bound in England by CPI UK

For a complete list of Pen & Sword titles, please contact
Pen & Sword Books Limited
47 Church Street, Barnsley, South Yorkshire, S70 2AS, England
E-mail: enquiries@pen-and-sword.co.uk
Website: www.pen-and-sword.co.uk

Contents

List of Illustrations

Maps

Editor's Note

Old Style and New Style Calendars

The sixteenth century saw deep religious divisions across Europe, reflected by the different calendars then in use. Those nations loyal to Rome, including Spain, had adopted the Gregorian calendar – named after Pope Gregory XIII (1572–85) – in the 1580s; but Protestant countries, including England, continued to use the Julian calendar for the next 100 years or so: thus remaining ten days behind their Catholic neighbours. In general, the dates in this book are given in the Gregorian mode, but where contemporary English sources use the old Julian form, the Gregorian equivalent is given in brackets with NS, for 'New Style'.

The Weather-Gauge

The windward position (i.e., the side from which the wind is blowing) in relation to another ship or fleet. Gaining the weather-gauge was a crucial combat advantage to the sailing ships of the day, offering, as it did, increased speed and manoeuvrability.

Background

Little more than thirty years before the Armada sailed in 1588, few would have anticipated war between England and Spain. The earlier Tudor monarchs had maintained amicable relations with their Spanish counterparts, united by distrust of their common neighbour, France.

Relations were strained when Henry VIII divorced his Spanish wife, Catherine of Aragon, and in defiance of the pope established the Church of England with himself as its head. But the accession of his eldest daughter, the devoutly Catholic Mary, in 1553 not only brought England back to Rome but in

Propaganda: a typical depiction of religion-inspired atrocities, in this case perpetrated by Protestants.

Philip II (1527–98). The king's austere style of dress reflects the increasing rigour of his outlook in the later years of his reign.

1554 seemed to herald the union of the two kingdoms when King Philip II of Spain married Queen Mary.

However, the Spaniards were generally unpopular in England, and the loss in 1558 of Calais as a result of English involvement in Spain's war with France soured relations still further, while the death of the still childless Mary spelt the end of any faint chance of an Anglo-Spanish union.

Half-hearted proposals that Philip marry England's new ruler, the former Princess Elizabeth, daughter of Henry VIII and his second wife, Anne Boleyn, came to nothing, but for some years relations between England and Spain, while growing cooler, seemed unlikely to degenerate into war. The situation, however, gradually changed.

Deepening Conflict

By the 1560s Philip II was ruler of a vast empire, including Spain, Naples, Sicily, the East Indies, possessions in the Americas and the Netherlands. The Spanish economy was increasingly dependent upon the resources of her New World

Deepening Conflict

Elizabeth I (1533–1603). A depiction of the queen in the later years of her reign, which is probably a more realistic impression than some of the more idealised portraits of Elizabeth.

settlements, particularly their gold and silver, but English traders quickly moved to exploit the opportunities presented by Spanish America, finding ready markets for their merchandise. Philip resented this, and on occasion took bloody action against those attempting to break Spanish monopolies in the region. In 1568 Spanish warships at San Juan d'Ulloa surprised and captured most of a squadron of English trading ships commanded by John Hawkins, merchant and slaver, and his young kinsman, Francis Drake.

The subsequent uproar in England forced Elizabeth to retaliate. Other factors were also troubling the queen and her ministers. In 1566, the northern, predominantly Protestant, Dutch provinces of the Netherlands had rebelled against Spain, and though the revolt had been bloodily crushed by the Duke of Alba, tensions remained high. Elizabeth – whose desire not to 'make windows upon men's hearts and secret thoughts' – had a deep distrust of all rebels, but she gave some indirect aid to the Dutch by seizing Spanish ships carrying 160,000 ducats, intended as pay for the Spanish Army of Flanders. This act was ostensibly a reprisal for the attack on Hawkins.

Pirates and Privateers

The exploits of Francis Drake, Walter Raleigh, and other Elizabethan seadogs on the Spanish Main are often seen as one of the more romantic aspects of the Anglo-Spanish war. The reality was often rather different.

The legal definitions of a 'privateer' – someone licensed by a government to operate against that country's enemies – and a 'pirate' – a freebooter who preyed more or less indiscriminately on shipping of various nationalities – often became blurred. This was due, in part, to a degree of ambivalence of the part of Elizabeth towards her privateers, which was reciprocated, in turn, by the seadogs themselves.

The first raiders to operate against Philip II's possessions in the New World were French, with English seamen – originally present in the region as traders – not joining the onslaught till after the Spanish attack on John Hawkins' squadron at San Juan d'Ulloa in 1569. It was with the proclaimed intention of seeking revenge for this assault that Francis Drake and a number of other adventurers began attacks on Spanish settlements and shipping during the 1570s.

The uncertain legal status of these raiders was underlined by the surreptitious financial backing – in return for a major share of the profits – sometimes given by the queen, and more openly by consortiums of gentry and merchants. For most of the decade following 1570, however, despite the headline-stealing exploits of Francis Drake, English privateering operations in the Caribbean were conducted on a fairly small scale, with minimal impact.

The overriding attraction for privateers – both then and later – was the fabled treasures of the Spanish gold and silver mines. They dreamt of taking one of the fabulous treasure fleets or *flotas* but although the Dutch captured one later in the century, the English were never successful. Attacks on the land convoy routes across the Panama Isthmus to the embarkation point at Nombre de Dios also met with minimal success: although Drake succeeded in taking part of one such mule train in 1573. It is a measure of the relative failure of the privateers that during the period between 1540 and 1650 the generally highly effective Spanish convoy system only lost an annual average of 0.5 per cent of their ships to enemy action. Symbolically perhaps, the last great raid by Drake and Hawkins, in 1595, ended in failure, with both commanders dying of disease in the course of the expedition.

In fact, it was during the later years of the war that English attacks at sea had an appreciable impact. These operations were largely the work of a new generation of seamen, aided by a growing fleet of specially built, privately owned men-of-war. These commanders, and the consortiums that often financed them, were increasingly unconcerned about the exact legal status of their operations. They were effectively given a free hand by Elizabeth, whose ministers commented that 'Her Majesty shall not venture to espy the faults of those that will venture their own to do her service.' This was a war whose aim was profit, with little regard for the means by which it was obtained. Contrary to popular belief, most privateers operated not in the Caribbean, but in the Eastern Atlantic and off the British coast. Their attacks were frequently indiscriminate, with Dutch, Scottish, Scandinavian, and Polish ships all being seized on the pretext that they were carrying goods bound for Spain.

But these attacks also did considerable damage to Spanish shipping, and together with continued raids in the New World, struck an ultimately far more serious blow to the Spanish economy than the defeat of the Armada ever did, taking and sinking, in the course of the war, some 1,000 Spanish vessels, their booty providing a major boost for English coffers.

But in the following years another problem brought Spain and England ever closer to the brink. In 1567 the Catholic Mary, Queen of Scots, was deposed by a group of Protestant Scottish nobles and took refuge in England, where she proved to be an increasing danger to Elizabeth. As the granddaughter of Henry VIII's sister, Mary was heir to the English throne, and was regarded by many Catholics in England – and almost universally in Catholic Europe – as the rightful Queen of England, while Elizabeth was regarded merely as the illegitimate issue of Henry and Anne Boleyn, whose marriage had never been recognised by Rome.

Virtually from the moment she arrived in England, Mary became the centre of plotting by disaffected English Catholics, covertly supported by Spain. Elizabeth, while fearful of provoking Philip into open conflict, responded by tacitly encouraging English privateers (commerce raiders licensed by their government) such as Drake and Martin Frobisher in their raids against Spanish shipping and settlements in the New World – in return for a share of the plunder.

In 1572, with unofficial English logistical support, Dutch rebels – known as the Sea Beggars – seized several Dutch ports, re-igniting the uprising against Spain. Though Elizabeth shied away from giving the rebels open recognition, she allowed English volunteers to fight alongside them, and Philip was forced to commit increasing numbers of troops and resources in an effort to contain the rebellion. In 1578, Philip reinforced the Army of Flanders and placed it under the command of his talented nephew, Alexander Farnese, Duke of Parma.

Background

Sir Francis Drake (c.1540–96). Drake's rise from humble origins is signified here by the prominent place given to his coat of arms. The renderings of the globe allude to his circumnavigation of the world (1579–80).

Although Parma was able to contain the insurgents, he came to feel that only by removing English support could the rebel provinces finally be subdued.

Elizabeth's sea dogs, meanwhile, were growing bolder. Between 1577 and 1580 Francis Drake carried out his epic circumnavigation of the globe, during which he attacked Spanish shipping and settlements across the world. Far from accepting Spanish demands that he be punished as a pirate, Elizabeth, on Drake's return, signalled her support for his actions by knighting him on the deck of his ship, *Golden Hind*. Once again she expected a handsome share of booty.

In the same year open war came a step closer when Spanish ships under an experienced commander, Juan Martinez de Recalde, landed Spanish and Papal 'volunteers' at Smerwick in Ireland to support an Irish uprising against English rule. The invaders were defeated and massacred, but enmity between England

Sir Martin Frobisher (c.1537–94). A tough man and a notable fighter. During the 1560s he was a privateer, and possibly a pirate. In the following decade he made three voyages of exploration in search of the North West Passage between the Atlantic and the Pacific.

and Spain had been inflamed further.

Philip significantly expanded his power when, in 1580, he annexed Portugal. As well as its overseas empire, he gained control of the major Atlantic port of Lisbon and the small but powerful Portuguese fleet. In response, England and France provided unofficial naval support to the pretender to the Portuguese throne in his attempt to hold the islands of the Azores. But in 1582 Spain demonstrated its growing strength at sea when a fleet under Philip's most experienced naval commander, Don Alvaro de Bazan, 1st Marquis of Santa Cruz, routed the rebel fleet and its French and English auxiliaries at the Battle of Sao Miguel, and in the following year captured the rebel base at Terceira.

Planning an Invasion

Although no English ships had been captured, Philip felt that the victory at São Miguel demonstrated that Elizabeth's sailors could be defeated, and for the first

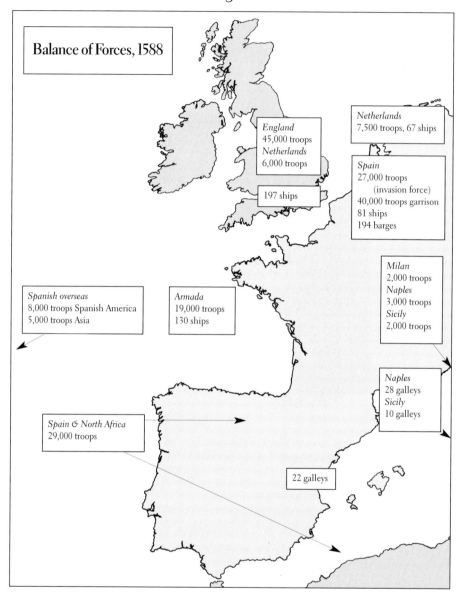

Balance of Forces, 1588

England
45,000 troops
Netherlands
6,000 troops

197 ships

Netherlands
7,500 troops, 67 ships

Spain
27,000 troops
 (invasion force)
40,000 troops garrison
81 ships
194 barges

Milan
2,000 troops
Naples
3,000 troops
Sicily
2,000 troops

Spanish overseas
8,000 troops Spanish America
5,000 troops Asia

Armada
19,000 troops
130 ships

Naples
28 galleys
Sicily
10 galleys

Spain & North Africa
29,000 troops

22 galleys

time began seriously to contemplate an invasion of England. The task of devising a plan and preparing a fleet was entrusted to Santa Cruz. The latter, foreseeing the difficulties involved, reacted cautiously, demanding a massive naval force to carry out the undertaking.

The bulk of the troops required would come from Parma's Army of Flanders. Parma assured Philip that if he could make a surprise landing, London would fall within eight days. However, as the king noted, Parma's precondition of taking the

Planning an invasion

Alessandro Farnese, Duke of Parma (1544–92). As well as being an extremely capable soldier, Parma was a noted patron of the arts. He died after being wounded at the Siege of Rouen in 1592.

English by surprise was incompatible with his requirement for 700 invasion craft. Philip put forward his own compromise plan, by which Santa Cruz and his armada would carry out diversionary landings in Ireland and possibly Wales, drawing off the English fleet and allowing Parma to make his crossing. Philip – who allegedly feared war 'as a burnt child dreads the fire' – hoped in this way to avoid having to fight a major naval action.

Preparations continued slowly and Philip remained hesitant. But in 1585, a string of victories by Parma against the Dutch rebels forced Elizabeth's hand. With France weakened and divided by the ongoing Wars of Religion between Catholics and Protestant Huguenots, Spain was coming dangerously near to total supremacy in Western Europe, and with the ports of the Dutch coast firmly in her hands, would be in a position to launch an overwhelming attack on England. So in August 1585, swallowing her doubts, Elizabeth signed the Treaty of

Nonesuch with the rebel Dutch provinces, by which she was bound to supply financial assistance, and the support of a 7,000-strong English army under the Earl of Leicester.

At roughly the same time, Drake's largest operation to date in Spanish America was climaxing in the sack of Santo Domingo, which occurred in December 1584.

Although open war had now effectively begun, Philip hesitated at the prospect of replacing Elizabeth with Mary, Queen of Scots. Though she was otherwise highly suitable, Mary's first husband had been King of France, and she remained strongly pro-French in her outlook. Philip had no desire to place on the English throne a monarch who would take that country into a French alliance.

To avoid this, the king considered marrying Mary to Parma. But Philip was not entirely sure of Parma's loyalty either. There were rumours that Elizabeth was attempting to subvert him with offers of the throne of the Netherlands, and there could be no certainty that as consort of Mary, and effective ruler of England, Parma would prove amenable to Philip's control.

But, true to Philip's tendency to procrastinate in the hope that time would solve problems for him, events now played into his hands. In 1586, Elizabeth's intelligence agencies – directed by the fiercely anti-Catholic Sir Francis Walsingham – uncovered the latest Catholic conspiracy in support of Queen Mary. The 'Babington Plot', involving the assassination of Elizabeth, had, as usual, been promised Spanish support. More importantly, the evidence deeply implicated Mary. Armed with this proof, Elizabeth's councillors at last prevailed on the reluctant monarch to agree to Mary's trial, and subsequently to her execution, which took place on 18 February 1587.

Elizabeth's reluctance to remove Mary had been due, in part, to the realisation that her death would simplify things for Philip: it would enrage Catholic Europe, and give Philip the possibility of spiritual approval and financial aid from the pope, in a 'crusade' against Protestant England and its 'witch queen'.

Grand Strategy

Philip's plans now moved ahead more rapidly. Santa Cruz's original proposals had demanded a massive fleet of over 500 ships, carrying almost 100,000 men, including 65,000 soldiers. This expedition, which would have operated independently from Parma's Army of Flanders, was clearly beyond Spanish resources, so all discussions now centred around the joint use of an armada from Spain and troops from the Netherlands: some 30,000 of whom Parma reckoned on being able to land on the English coast between Margate and Dover in the space of eight to twelve hours. Unlike Philip, who was unduly influenced by the optimistic assurances of English exiles, Parma placed no reliance on being supported by a

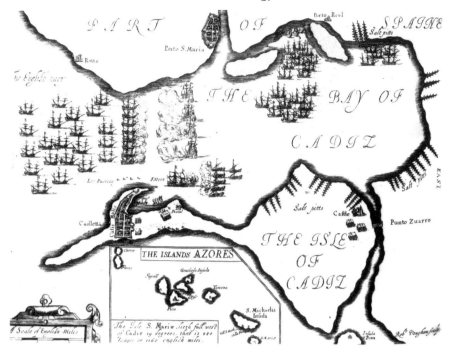

Cadiz Harbour. A near-contemporary English view, probably depicting the attack made in 1596.

rising of English Catholics.

Throughout the opening months of 1587 ships, men and supplies continued to be gathered at Lisbon. The port of Cadiz in Andalusia was an important staging post where the Duke of Medina Sidonia skilfully orchestrated the rendezvous of ships and stores from Southern Spain and the Mediterranean before despatching them to Santa Cruz at Lisbon.

By early April, English reports suggested that around sixty ships were gathered at Cadiz, and Elizabeth's leading seamen implored her to permit a pre-emptive strike against them, in order to 'smoke the wasps out of their nests'. Such an attack would make full-scale war inevitable, and Elizabeth hesitated before giving Drake authority to take his squadron, including four of the Queen's Ships (regular warships of the Navy Royal), to strike at Cadiz on 12 April. Typically, she then attempted to modify her permission, but Drake was safely away, and on 29 April his squadron stormed Cadiz harbour, burning and sinking twenty-four to thirty-seven of the ships anchored there, and destroying the stores which they carried. Drake commented that he had 'singed the King of Spain's beard', which was not in fact the boast it is sometimes represented as being, for

Background

Drake's implication was that beards soon grow again. However, the attack – augmented by a further six weeks of raiding along the Spanish and Portuguese coast – ensured the Armada would not sail that year.

Philip repeatedly urged Santa Cruz to sail with what ships he had available, but the Marquis, distracted for much of the summer by the need to safeguard the *flota* (the fleet bringing treasure and other goods) from the Indies against attack by Drake, knew his best ships needed refitting after the wear and tear of their operations. By now both Santa Cruz and Parma – otherwise frequently at odds with each other – were becoming noticeably less optimistic in their assessments of the likely success of the Spanish plan. At Lisbon, unbeknown to King Philip, whose repeated demands for haste were proving fruitless, near chaos reigned, as supplies for the Armada rotted on the docksides and men deserted or fell sick. In the Low Countries, Parma's *tercios* (army units of roughly 3,000 men each) dwindled as his troops fell victim to disease.

By early January 1588, the Armada was still not ready for sea, and an increasingly anxious Philip was about to order an investigation when Santa Cruz effectively opted out of the expedition by falling ill and dying. The king rather unfeelingly commented: 'God has shown me favour by removing the Marquis now rather than when the Armada is at sea,' and appointed as Santa Cruz's successor perhaps the most reviled figure in the whole story of the Armada: Don Alonso Perez de Guzman, 7th Duke of Medina Sidonia.

As we shall see later, despite his own protestations of unsuitability, Medina Sidonia was in many ways the natural choice to command the Armada: and while he and his squadron commanders worked feverishly – and with some success – to sort out the administrative mayhem that had greeted him on his arrival at Lisbon in February 1588, the final touches were being made to Spanish strategy for the assault on England.

Leaks from various sources had by now revealed to the English at least the broad outlines of the plan devised by Santa Cruz and Parma, and the latter's idea of making a surprise crossing of the Channel was certainly no longer feasible. It was equally apparent that with the ships – approximately 130 – he was likely to muster, Medina Sidonia would be unable to transport enough troops to carry out the invasion unaided. A joint operation was therefore essential, and it was at this point that Spanish planning began to encounter difficulties.

With Parma in Brussels and Medina Sidonia in Lisbon, direct communication was clearly difficult, and as a result King Philip and his immediate advisers undertook to coordinate planning. As soon became apparent, this arrangement was rife with possibilities for misunderstanding.

Parma was now displaying a distinct lack of enthusiasm for the whole project. It has been suggested he had originally been motivated in his support by the

The Escorial Palace: Philip II's semi-monastical retreat.

prospect of obtaining reinforcements for his Army of Flanders, and that when he realised the Armada was a serious proposition, he developed cold feet.

The plan that evolved during the early months of 1588 now envisaged the Armada making its way up-Channel, making a rendezvous with Parma, and escorting his barges to their landing point between Dover and Margate. Then, reinforced by 9,000 of Medina Sidonia's troops, Parma's invasion force, which had shrunk through a winter of attrition to about 18,000 men – instead of the 30,000 originally intended – would march swiftly on London, its flank supported by the Armada in the Thames Estuary. With Elizabeth and her ministers dead, taken, or fled, Parma might be in a position to complete the subjugation of England and the installation of a pro-Spanish regime, perhaps nominally headed by Philip's daughter, the Infanta Isabella. In practice, both Parma and Philip had serious doubts about the feasibility of actually conquering the whole of England, and Parma was secretly authorised to offer compromise terms, involving a war indemnity, toleration for English Catholics, and non-interference by England in the affairs of the Netherlands.

But a scheme which, in the quiet solitude of his study in the Escorial (the great monastery-palace north of Madrid) might have seemed eminently workable to Philip, actually contained major difficulties. Severe restrictions were placed upon Medina Sidonia's freedom of action. He was not to seek out an engagement with the English fleet – though dismissed by Philip as 'inferior' – until after he had linked up with Parma. He was especially debarred from taking the sensible course of securing an English port or anchorage – such as Plymouth or the Solent near the Isle of Wight – as a base of operations or alternative bridgehead. Only if the rendezvous with Parma proved impossible was Medina Sidonia permitted to attempt the capture of the Isle of Wight.

But the greatest problem, and source of misunderstanding, lay in the details of the proposed rendezvous between Parma and Medina Sidonia. The latter assumed that Parma's invasion fleet would put out from its bases at Nieuport and Dunkirk, and link up with the Armada either just off the Flanders coast or in mid-Channel. But Parma was now expressing serious doubts whether such a plan was feasible. He pointed out to the king, accurately enough, that an English naval squadron was stationed in the Channel with the mission of intercepting him. This, might, of course, be dealt with by the Armada. But even more of a threat was presented by the Dutch flotilla of shallow-draught crompsters and fly-boats, under Justin of Nassau, which maintained a fairly continuous blockade in the coastal waters off the invasion ports. As we shall see later, Parma seems to have exaggerated his difficulties in a letter of 22 June to the king, but they were real enough:

'With regard to my going out to join [Medina Sidonia], he will plainly see that with these little, low, flat boats, built for the rivers and not for the sea, I cannot change from the short direct passage across which was agreed upon. It will be a great mercy of God, indeed if, even when our passage is pro-tected and the Channel free from the enemy's vessels, we are able to reach land in these boats... If I were to attempt such a thing by going out to meet the duke, and we came across any of the armed English or rebel ships, they could destroy us with the greatest of ease. This must be obvious, and neither the valour of our men nor any other human effort could save us.'

Although Philip seems to have realised Parma's latest views conflicted sharply with those of Medina Sidonia, he does not appear to have alerted the Armada's commander to the discrepancy. Instead, he convinced himself that God would provide a solution to the obvious failings in the Spanish strategy, telling Medina Sidonia:

'Victory is a gift from God. He grants it, or takes it away as He wills. Since you are in charge of executing His work, we can expect Him to assist us, unless we become unworthy of this through our sins.'

Even if Medina Sidonia was comforted by this view, which is debatable, it cut little ice with his more seasoned officers. It was probably one of these, Juan

Trained Bands and Militia

The exact definitions of these staples of England's defence on land have often been the cause of much confusion, especially as the terms were frequently mis-applied even by contemporaries. In broad terms, the militia, or *posse comitatus*, consisted of a county's entire able-bodied male population, between the ages of sixteen and sixty. Although it was rare for all to be levied, this system had formed the basis of home defence for much of the medieval period.

The Tudor regime, with its fears of internal dissent and insurrection – and also influenced by the cost of modern arms and equipment – set up a new internal defence force, known as the trained bands in 1573. As well as providing a defence against external attack, the trained bands were intended to be recruited from the 'better sort' of more substantial men, who might be felt to have a stake in maintaining internal order and stability.

The trained bands, like the militia, which continued in at least notional existence, were organised by county. Reluctant to entrust too much power to the nobility, Elizabeth put the trained bands in the charge of each county's lord lieutenant and his deputies. They, in turn, appointed muster-masters – usually professional soldiers – to undertake the training of 'corporals', who in turn, instructed the local companies at meetings: the frequency of which varied according to the perceived level of external threat current at the time.

Each county's trained bands, whose men were usually expected to purchase their own equipment according to their financial status, held annual general musters, which were often the occasion as much for jollification as for military exercises.

Trained bands varied considerably in their actual level training and effectiveness. Some, such as the trained bands of the City of London, which were financed by wealthy merchants and operated under the close eye of the Crown, were regarded as proficient and reliable troops. Others, particularly in poorer or more remote regions, were woefully equipped and ill-prepared. In general terms, very few of them were likely to have provided real opposition to the veterans of the Army of Flanders.

Charles Howard, Lord Effingham, later Earl of Nottingham (1536–1624). Though not an experienced naval commander, several members of the Howard family had previously held the post of Lord Admiral. Charles proved a competent administrator, though not outstanding as a fleet commander.

Martinez Recalde, who, after listing some of the weaknesses of the Spanish strategy to a representative of the pope, concluded sardonically: 'So we are sailing in the confident hope of a miracle.'

Opening Moves

The English strategic response to the Spanish threat was at once simpler and more difficult. Elizabeth and her ministers were keenly aware that if the veterans of the Army of Flanders once established a bridgehead, the numerically large but poorly trained and equipped English land forces centred around the trained bands and militia would be no match for them. With few modern fortifications to delay Parma, the most the English could realistically aim at was to fight a rearguard action, combined with a scorched earth policy, in the hope of wearing down the invader.

England's main hopes lay at sea. During the early months of 1588 there was debate between those of the queen's counsellors who favoured concentrating the fleet in the Straits of Dover, in order to contest a crossing by Parma, and those – mainly seamen headed by Drake and later the lord admiral, Charles Howard – who favoured a forward defence policy, with the fleet engaging the Armada as close to its own ports as possible. In the end, largely because of Drake's forceful advocacy – pointing out that 'the water-gates of England are the ports of the enemy,' while 'The advantage of time and place in all martial actions is half the victory, which being lost is irrecoverable' – a compromise was reached. The bulk of the fleet, under Howard and Drake, would be stationed at Plymouth, to pursue the 'forward' strategy, while a smaller, but still powerful, squadron under Lord Henry Seymour, remained in the Straits of Dover in rather half-hearted co-operation with the Dutch.

In the event the Armada reached the Channel anyway, the strategy of the Plymouth force would be to gain the weather-gauge (the advantage of the wind direction), by taking up station to the west of the Armada, employing the generally prevailing westerly winds, and harry it up-Channel: giving Medina Sidonia no opportunity to secure a landing-place, and eventually trapping him between Howard, Drake, and Seymour.

Opening Moves

Medina Sidonia eventually sailed with about 130 ships, carrying 29,453 men, of whom about 19,000 were soldiers and the remainder seamen, volunteers, and auxiliaries of various kinds.

Howard would at various times have some 197 ships under his command, crewed by around 15,900 men, most of them seamen. Many, however, only joined the English fleet in the later stages of the campaign.

On shore, the Duke of Parma had in the region of 17,000 men, drawn from the Army of Flanders, designated to form his invasion force. He would be opposed by a mixed English force composed of volunteers, the retinues of some of the leading nobility, and county trained bands and militias, whose numbers fluctuated continually. But while they theoretically outnumbered Parma

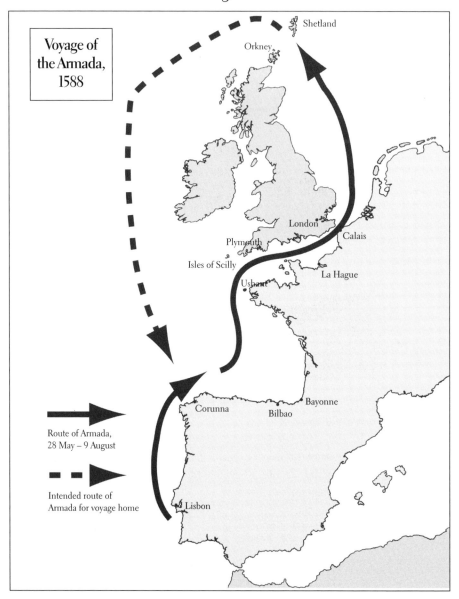

Voyage of
the Armada,
1588

Shetland

Orkney

London

Plymouth

Calais

Isles of Scilly

Ushant

La Hague

Corunna

Bayonne

Bilbao

Lisbon

Route of Armada,
28 May – 9 August

Intended route of
Armada for voyage home

considerably, the vast majority could in no way be compared to the Spanish veterans in terms of training, equipment, or experience.

Much has been written about the differences in shipbuilding and design, armament, and tactics which distinguished the rival fleets but this can only be summarised here.

The bulk of the ships comprising the Armada – even its first-line squadrons – were not purpose-built fighting ships. Only the galleons of the Portuguese

Spanish troops in flat-bottomed boats.

Squadron and to a lesser extent those of Castile, together with the four galleasses of Naples, can really be described as such. The rest were commandeered merchant ships and grain carriers, whose effectiveness was variable. In general terms, the majority of the warships that served with the Armada, whether galleons, or armed merchantmen, were mostly of the type known as *naos*, which, while similar in tonnage to many of their opponents, appeared larger because of their high superstructures. This factor also made them less manoeuvrable and responsive than both the queen's ships and many of the auxiliary craft with Howard, many of which were built as privateers.

The most effective of the English vessels were the 'race-built' galleons, which were either built as such from scratch or remodelled and formed the bulk of the queen's ships. The term 'race-built', does not, as occasionally thought, refer to their speed and manoeuvrability, but to their lower superstructures and clean hull design, which did indeed give them advantages of speed and seaworthiness over their opponents, and equally importantly, made them highly effective floating gun platforms. For it was the firepower of the opposing fleets, and the tactics they

Spanish galleys.

employed, which would prove to be the decisive factor.

It is often said that Spanish tactics consisted of trying to close with their opponents, then grapple, board, and overwhelm them with the large numbers of soldiers most of the Armada ships carried. The English, on the other hand, are said to have stood off and battered their opponents with cannon from a distance. While there is an element of truth in this, the actual situation was more complex.

'Race-Built' Galleons

The success of the English fleet is often attributed to their superiority in ship design, in particular to their 'race-built' galleons. The 'race-built' galleon appears to date from around 1578, when John Hawkins became treasurer of the Navy. Compared with earlier galleons, including those of the Spanish, the 'race-built' galleons were longer in relation to their beam, with finer underwater lines. Their fore and stern castles were reduced in height, while their improved sail plans added to their speed and manoeuvrability. Their continuous lower decks, running the length of the ship, were specially designed to house heavy guns.

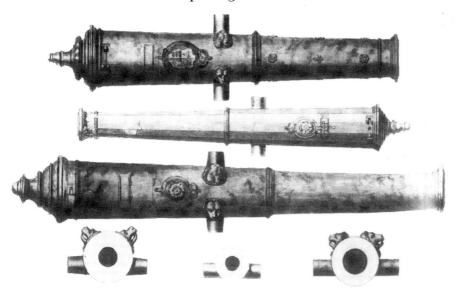

Types of cannon, including a demi-cannon (top), a demi-culverin (centre), and a full cannon (below).

The Spaniards indeed hoped to employ the tactics summarised above, but as witnessed during the fighting in the Azores, they could also employ artillery as their primary weapon. Indeed, before the Spaniards set out, they were aware of the likely tactics the English would employ against them; and that they, too, might have to rely on their guns to force a decision.

But it was in gunnery, as well as manoeuvrability, that the English had the edge on the Spaniards. There have been many attempts to assess the relative merits of the guns carried by the antagonists: the table below (p. 69) summarises the main ordnance of the opposing fleets.

A significant factor was the English numerical advantage in demi-culverins, which were the longest-ranged pieces on either side. In practice, however, as the English recognised after the initial engagements, they were only really effective as ship-smashers at a range of under 400 yards. As a result, English tactics trod a fine line between getting near enough to the enemy to inflict serious damage, while at the same time avoiding coming close enough to be grappled and boarded. In this, their manoeuvrability gave them a clear edge over most vessels of the Armada.

But the English possessed another advantage, which proved decisive. Spanish guns were mounted on old two-wheeled gun carriages, which were usually lashed to the side of the ship to absorb recoil. It was difficult to manhandle inboard for reloading, and often resulted in a gunner having to reload 'outboard', awkwardly straddling the barrel and exposed to enemy fire. Spanish ships carried fewer trained gunners than their English counterparts, and while the gunners loaded and sighted each piece, the actual gun-handling was carried out by soldiers. The outcome was a painfully slow rate of fire, often amounting to no more than one shot per gun per hour, once the initial, previously loaded, broadside had been fired. English guns, however, were mounted on four-wheeled carriages secured by ropes and pulleys, which allowed them to be drawn inboard for reloading. With more gunners and better-trained crews, the outcome was a much faster rate of fire than the Spaniards: perhaps three or four shots per hour.

In terms of commanders, neither Medina Sidonia nor Howard had great experience at sea, both being appointed, at least partly, from social considerations. Both, however, proved ready to listen to advice from more seasoned subordinates. And while veteran sea dogs such as Drake and Frobisher spring readily to mind, the Armada could also boast seasoned commanders, like Recalde, Bertendona, and Oquendo. The English captains, however, had the advantage of detailed knowledge of the waters in which the campaign would be fought.

Although, overall, the English ships were crewed by seamen more experienced than their opponents in the ways of the North Atlantic and the waters surrounding Britain, a high proportion of Spanish seamen had sailed the Atlantic to the Indies or the Newfoundland fisheries: in the event, only those with little experience of northern waters – and of course, raw recruits, would be at a serious disadvantage.

Command and Control

The Spanish

Overall responsibility for planning and general conduct of the campaign rested with King Philip II, together with one or two of his closest advisers. The king continued to be as closely involved as possible in decision-making. The naval element of the enterprise was commanded by the Duke of Medina Sidonia, while the actual invasion force, drawn from the Army of Flanders, was led by the Duke of Parma.

Though not very clearly established, it appears that when the two forces united, Medina Sidonia was to exercise overall command until the expedition made landfall in England. At this point, the Duke of Parma would assume control of land operations, while the fleet remained under Medina Sidonia.

Unlike land forces, where some definite hierarchy of command was by now appearing, the situation in naval forces of the period was still considerably more ill-defined than in modern times. Particularly in this campaign, it is often hard to discover how command and control on a fleet level was actually

The Galleass

These vessels, in theory, combined the firepower of the galleon with the manoeuvrability of the oar-powered fighting ship. They were first used in the 1530s by the Venetians, and copied by the Spaniards. The Venetian galleasses were 152 feet long by 26 feet in the beam, and carried a mixture of square and lateen sails. They had twenty-eight banks of oars, mainly manned by convicts or enemy prisoners of war, and carried a complement of 250 soldiers and seventy sailors.

The Neapolitan galleass squadron serving with the Armada made a strong impression on their English opponents, confirmed by the prominent place they are given in most contemporary illustrations of the campaign. One English eyewitness described them thus: 'The oars all red, the sails had upon them the bloody sword; the upper part of the galleass was also red...' To add to the effect, the rowers had been issued with red jackets.

The role of the galleasses was to bring heavy firepower to bear in situations where ordinary sailing vessels could not operate. For this purpose, the *capitana*, *San Lorenzo*, had six heavy pieces, ranging from 15- to 50-pounders, mounted in her bows, and four more in her stern. About twenty more guns, of various calibres, were ranged in her fore and stern castles, and another twenty lighter breech-loading guns were positioned, ten to a side, above her oar decks. In a gesture to the role of the galley in classical warfare, each galleass was also fitted with a large iron ram.

Opinions differed on the effectiveness of the galleasses. In general their performance under oars proved disappointing. But they were often involved in the thick of the action, and were treated with a good deal of respect by their English opponents. They had, however, one fatal weakness. The design of their rudders and their fittings to the hull were inadequate: as a result of this, two galleasses were lost and a third eventually drifted ashore in France, never to sail again.

exercised in battle.

When looking at the organisation of the Armada, and how it was commanded in action, it is important to realise that 'squadrons' were primarily administrative units, named after their area of origin, rather than distinct fighting flotillas: although the galleass squadron was generally treated as a discrete combat entity.

The common practice was to form 'battlegroups' or *socorros*, not necessarily confined to ships of one squadron, and indeed very flexible in their composition. Their leaders were generally also squadron commanders: with the exception of

Background

Don Alonso de Leiva, who had been nominated by the king as successor to Medina Sidonia as captain-general in the event of the latter's death or incapacity. Recalde was senior squadron commander, and acted as second in command of the Armada: though during the days following Gravelines, when Medina Sidonia briefly failed to exercise command, Recalde's illness resulted in Don Francisco de Bobadilla – the senior military commander with the Armada – shouldering much of the responsibility pending the duke's recovery. Diego Flores de Valdez was both a squadron commander and Medina Sidonia's professional adviser (or in modern parlance, chief of staff). In reality, however, despite spending most of the voyage occupied in this latter role, his powers were poorly defined.

In theory, all major decisions were taken after Medina Sidonia had consulted with his council of war, which consisted of the squadron commanders, de Leiva, and senior military officers. In practice, however, the duke (and Flores de Valdez) could, and sometimes did, override the opinion of the majority of the council.

Thus, with these provisos in mind, the theoretical command structure of the Armada was as follows:

Captain-General
    Duke of Medina Sidonia: commander of the Squadron of Portugal
Second in Command
    Juan Martinez de Recalde: commander of the Squadron of Biscay, though he did not sail with his squadron, which was probably commanded by its vice admiral, A. Felipe
Chief of Staff
    Diego Flores de Valdez: commander of the Squadron of Castile, though for most of the campaign command was probably exercised by its vice admiral, Martin Aramburu
Squadron Commanders
    Don Pedro de Valdez: Squadron of Andalusia, but succeeded on capture by Don Diego Tellez Enriquez
    Miguel de Oquendo: Squadron of Guipuzcoa
    Martin de Bertendona: Levant Squadron
    Juan Gomez de Medina: Squadron of Hulks
    Don Hugo de Moncada: Galleasses of Naples
    Don Antonio Hurtado de Mendoza: *Pataches* and *Zabras*
    Diego de Medrano: Galleys of Portugal
Army units on-board the Armada
    Don Francisco de Bobadilla: commanding some 19,000 men (about half of which were raw recruits), organised in five *tercios* and some independent companies.

Command and Control

The English

However ill-defined the Armada's command structure may have been, that of the English forces was initially even more informal. The fleet was divided into two squadrons. The larger, Western Squadron, based on Plymouth, was commanded until early June by Sir Francis Drake. However, England's senior naval commander, the lord admiral, Lord Charles Howard, then took over personal command of the Western Squadron, with Drake as his vice admiral.

We have no conclusive evidence as to how the Western Squadron was organised and led during its first two engagements off Plymouth and Portland Bill. It seems possible that it adopted a somewhat free-for-all approach, with the fleet roughly split between Howard and Drake, but with captains largely making their own choice as to which of the squadron's commanders they actually joined.

Such an arrangement was plainly unsatisfactory, and after the Portland Bill action Howard's force was reorganised into four squadrons under the lord admiral himself, Sir Francis Drake, Martin Frobisher and John Hawkins. Our knowledge of the composition of each squadron, and whether this was fixed or flexible, is incomplete. Each squadron probably consisted of a core of several Queen's Ships together with a number of large merchantmen, augmented by a fleet of smaller vessels – not all of which would have served for the whole of the campaign.

An English army on the march in Ireland. Most of the English troops in 1588 were not so well-equipped, and this engraving probably more accurately shows the appearance of the Army of Flanders.

Background

Robert Dudley, Earl of Leicester (?1532–88). Leicester, as Elizabeth's favourite, enjoyed her close confidence until his death. In the Netherlands, Leicester proved to be an indifferent general, despite which, he was placed in command of the forces mustered at Tilbury.

The 'Eastern', or 'Dover Straits', Squadron, while under Howard's overall control, was under the operational command of Lord Henry Seymour and his vice admiral, Sir William Wynter. These is some evidence to suggest that during the action off Gravelines, the squadron may have operated in two battlegroups or divisions under Seymour and Wynter.

Command and Control

It would be unrewarding to attempt a compilation of units that might, in theory, have served with the English land forces. Many would have been *ad hoc* bodies led by individual captains, gentry, and noblemen: although the county trained bands, which were supposedly available to contest any invasion, were organised into companies, usually based on, and named after, the towns or districts where they were raised.

Overall command was, in principle, exercised by Robert Dudley, Earl of Leicester, as the queen's lieutenant general. But until 2 August, his authority did not formally extend beyond Essex: and even thereafter, must have been nominal in most of the country, being effectively confined to the army raised for the defence of London and based at Tilbury. The Low Countries veteran, Sir John 'Black Jack' Norris, was general of the South-Eastern counties, and local commanders – such as Sir George Cary in the Isle of Wight, and Sir Thomas Scott in Kent – led the trained bands and other county-based units.

Armada 1588

Campaign Chronicle

---

6 February–9 May 1588: Medina Sidonia Takes Command

The Duke of Medina Sidonia's immediate reaction to being appointed as Santa Cruz's replacement seemed to border on panic. He wrote to King Philip, emphasising his unsuitability for the job: 'I have not health for the sea, for I know by the small experiences I have had afloat that I soon become sea-sick… Besides this, your Excellency knows, as I have often told you verbally and in writing, that I am in great need, so much so that when I have had to go to Madrid I have been obliged to borrow money for my journey… Apart from this, neither my conscience nor my duty will allow me to take this service upon me. The force is so great, and the undertaking so important, that it would not be right for a person like myself, possessing no experience of seafaring or of war, to take charge of it.'

Opinions differ as to Medina's Sidonia's real motives in making this protest, which, as he possibly expected, was ignored. It was quite customary for the captain-general of a Spanish fleet to be a man whose social standing considerably outweighed his experience of the sea. He would be expected to rely on professional advisers for assistance in that respect. The duke's real reasons may have been that, as result of his close involvement with the preparations already made, he was aware of the doubts about the expedition's prospects held by experienced commanders like Santa Cruz and Recalde, and was making his protest as a personal insurance against repercussions in the event of the failure he regarded as highly likely.

However, the initial task awaiting Medina Sidonia when he arrived at Lisbon was one suiting his proven abilities as an administrator. During the following weeks he worked hard to overcome the problems inherited from Santa Cruz with a fair degree of success. Guns, together with powder and shot, were redistributed more equally among the ships of the fleet, and stores – the quality of which, no one dared investigate too closely – loaded aboard the ships. The duke seems to have worked amicably with his squadron commanders, and issued detailed instructions regarding rations for his crews, covering what he must have felt to be

A typical sea-battle of the period.

every conceivable aspect, down to the order in which different wines were to be issued.

By early May, the Armada seemed as ready for sea as it was ever likely to be. Morale among many crews was high, with the men motivated by a mixture of the religious fervour emphasised in Medina Sidonia's final orders, and by the more mundane – if understandable – thoughts of the booty they would gather in a vanquished England. An unknown Spanish soldier aboard the Armada wrote to his wife:

'Your grace will say that she should commend me to God, for if there is

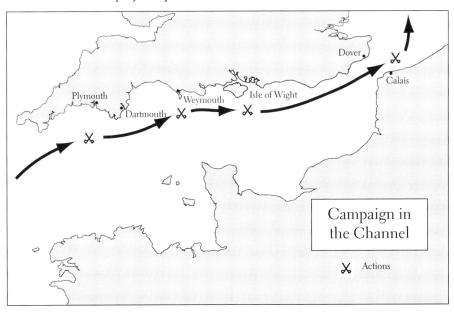

Campaign in the Channel

✂ Actions

one thing for which I wish to go on living, it is to return to her and to provide for her as by rights I ought, and if God gives me life, when this expedition to England is over, which will be very soon, I shall go back to my house again with whatever God shall be pleased to give me in order to have some peace. For it was for this that I came on this expedition, not because I am any lover of wandering away from home and God knows that all I want is to be there again in peace and with some little rest.'

On 9 May, after a colourful and impressive service of dedication in Lisbon Cathedral, Medina gave the order to weigh anchor and put to sea. His instructions to the men of the Armada were as follows:

'First and foremost, you must all know, from the highest to the lowest, that the principal reason which has moved His Majesty to undertake this enterprise is his desire to serve God, and to convert to his church many peoples and souls who are now oppressed by the heretical enemies of our Catholic faith.

'I also enjoin you to take particular care that no soldier, sailor or other person in the Armada shall blaspheme, or deny Our Lord, our Lady or the Saints, under very severe punishment inflicted at our discretion. With regard to other less serious oaths, the officers of the ships will do their best to repress their use, and will punish offenders by docking their wine ration; or in some other way at their discretion. As these disorders usually arise from gambling, you will endeavour to repress this as much as possible, especially the prohibited games, and allow no play at night on any account.

'As it is an evident inconvenience, as well as an offence to God, that public or other women should be permitted to accompany such an armada, I order that none should be taken on-board. If any attempt be made to embark women, I authorise the captains, and masters of ships to prevent it, and if it be done surreptitiously the offenders must be severely punished.

'Every morning at daybreak the ships' boys shall, as usual, say their "Salve", at the foot of the mainmast, and at sunset the "Ave Maria". Some days, and at least every Saturday, they shall say the "Salve" with the Litany.

'The ships will come to the flagship every evening to learn the watchword and receive orders… the flagship must be saluted by bugles if there are any on-board, or by fifes, and two cheers from the crews. When the response has been given the salute must be repeated. If the hour be late, the watchword must be requested, and when it has been obtained another salute must be given, and the ships will then make way for others.

'In case the weather should make it impossible to obtain the watchword on any days, the following words must be employed:

Sunday: Jesus
Monday: Holy Ghost
Tuesday: Most Holy Trinity
Wednesday: Santiago
Thursday: The Angels
Friday: All Saints
Saturday: Our Lady

'It is of great importance that the Armada should be kept well together, and the generals and chiefs of squadrons must endeavour to sail in as close order as possible… Great care and vigilance must be exercised to keep the squadron of hulks always in the midst of the fleet. The order about not preceding the flagship must be strictly obeyed, especially at night.

'No ship belonging to, or accompanying, the Armada shall separate from it without my permission. If any should be forced out of the course by tempest, before arriving off Cape Finisterre, they will make direct for that point, where they will find orders from me; but if no such orders be awaiting them, they will then make for Corunna, where they will receive orders. Any infraction of this order shall be punished by death and forfeiture.

'On leaving Cape Finisterre the course will be to the Scilly Isles, and ships must try to sight the islands from the south, taking great care to look to their soundings. If on the voyage any ships should get separated, they are not to return to Spain on any account, the punishment for disobedience being forfeiture and death with disgrace…'

10 May–19 June: From Lisbon to Corunna

The Armada, with its brightly-painted ships' hulls, glowing banners, and sounding trumpets, made a brave show as it left Lisbon harbour: but frustration quickly followed. For the next two weeks, held back by contrary winds, the fleet was unable to leave the mouth of the Tagus. On 14 May, Medina Sidonia wrote reassuringly to the king: 'the Armada took advantage of a light easterly wind, which blew for a few hours on the 11th instant, to drop down the river to Belem and Santa Catalina, where the ships now only await a fair wind to sail. God send it soon!' Ominously, just before sailing, Medina Sidonia had received a message from the Duke of Parma, written in March, from which it was apparent that Parma had fewer troops available than Medina Sidonia had expected – only about 17,000 – and that much of his invasion fleet was unready.

Medina Sidonia's worries mounted with every day the Armada remained windbound in the Tagus. The almost 30,000 men aboard his ships not only made serious inroads into the provisions intended for the voyage, but crammed together as they were in unsanitary conditions, disease spread rapidly and morale fell.

A Galleass. Note the high stern castle and the battery of guns mounted at the prow. An ornate stern lantern, similar to that seen here, was reportedly shot off a galleass during the engagement off the Isle of Wight.

Campaign Chronicle

Elizabethan ships, including a 'race-built' galleon.

At last, on 30 May, the winds turned favourable, allowing the Armada to begin moving out into the open sea. It was dawn next day before the last ship was clear, and soon afterwards the fleet ran into contrary freshening winds, followed by stormy weather, which forced the Armada to beat up and down, in the process losing most of the ground already gained. On 10 June, when the winds at last came into the NW direction favourable for the Spaniards, the fleet lay at latitude 40 degrees north – further from Cape Finisterre than when it had left Lisbon. On the same day Medina Sidonia wrote to Parma outlining his strategy for the coming campaign. The duke explained that he had been instructed to avoid battle, if possible, and make directly for a rendezvous with Parma: 'I very much wish the coast [of Flanders] were capable of sheltering so great a fleet as this, so that we might take a safe port to have at our backs, but as this is impossible, we shall have to make the best use we can of what accommodation there may be, and it will be necessary that as soon as Captain Moresin arrives with you (which will depend on the weather), you should come out to meet me...'

Parma was dismayed at the implications of Medina Sidonia's letter, and twelve days later wrote to the king that the captain-general of the Armada 'seems to have persuaded himself that I may be able to go out and meet him with my boats. These things cannot be.' Parma's flat-bottomed barges were barely fit for the short crossing of the English Channel in the Dover Straits, and were certainly incapable of making a longer voyage: 'This was one of the principal reasons which moved Your Majesty to lay down the precise and prudent orders you did, that your Spanish fleet should assure us the passage across, as it is perfectly clear that these boats could not contend against ships, much less stand the sea, for they will not weather the slightest storm.'

There is no record that Medina Sidonia ever learned of Parma's vitally important but discouraging letter. In any case, the Armada was now facing its own problems. By 17 June the fleet, sailing at an average speed of 4 knots, at last sighted Cape Finisterre at the north-west tip of Spain, but by now Medina Sidonia had discovered that a large proportion of the stores embarked at Lisbon were rotten and the water foul, with the result that dysentery had begun to spread among the crews. The duke was forced to admit to the king that the supplies 'have gone bad, rotted and spoiled... We have had to throw a large part of the food overboard because it was only giving men the plague and making them sick... So I must inform Your Majesty and humbly beg you to agree to send out to us more provisions to supplement what we have. What we mainly lack is meat and fish, but we need everything else as well.'

Then, as the Armada waited off Finisterre for the expected supply ships, further misfortune struck. Gales blew up, scattering the fleet over a wide area, some vessels being driven as far north as the Scilly Isles. With most of his fleet missing, Medina Sidonia was forced into the port of Corunna to wait for the stragglers to rejoin him.

Ensign Esquivel recounts the ordeal of his pinnace (a small vessel, propelled by oars or sails) in the storm:

'On Friday, 2 July, at daybreak we sighted St Michael's Bay [Mounts Bay, Cornwall] and Cape Longnose [the Lizard] 5 or 6 leagues distant. The general opinion was that, being so near the land, we should hardly fail to catch a fisherboat during the night. The wind then rose in the SW, with heavy squalls of rain, and such a violent gale that during the night we had winds from every quarter of the compass. We did our best by constant tacking to keep off the land, and at daybreak the wind settled in the N., and we tried to keep towards Ireland in order to fulfil our intention, but the wind was too strong, and the sea so heavy that the pinnace shipped a quantity of water at every wave. We ran thus in a southerly direction, with the wind astern blowing a gale, so that we could only carry our foresail very low. At four o'clock in the afternoon, after we had already received several heavy seas, a wave passed clean over us, and nearly swamped the pinnace. We were flush with the water, and almost lost, but by great effort of all hands the water was baled out, and everything thrown overboard. We had previously thrown over a pipe of wine and two butts of water. We lowered the mainmast on to the deck, and so we lived through the night under a closely reefed foresail.

'On Sunday we were running under the foresail only, and at nine o'clock in the morning we sighted six sails, three to the N., and three to the SE, although they appeared to be all of one company. We ran between them with our foresail set, and two of those on the SE gave us chase. We then hoisted our mainmast and clapped on sail, and after they had followed us until two o'clock, they took in sail and resumed their course. At nine o'clock we sighted another ship lying to and repairing, with only her lower sails set.

'On Monday, 4 July, we sighted land off Rivadeo [Northern Spain].'

20 June–23 July: Final Preparations

Various storm-blown stragglers from the Armada were sighted off the Scillies, and their presence gave Elizabeth and her commanders final proof, if such were needed, that the Spanish onslaught was imminent. Since early in the year, despite continued procrastination by the queen herself, the tempo of English preparations had been increasing. Drake, in command of the Western Squadron at Plymouth, constantly urged that the English fleet should launch a pre-emptive attack on Spanish ports.

While some of her privy council agreed with Drake, the queen herself remained reluctant to act. Sir Francis was still pressing his case early in June when the lord admiral, Charles Howard, arrived at Plymouth to assume overall command. Howard officially hoisted his standard on 2 June. Drake's reaction at being superseded by a courtier commander – though from a family with a long-standing naval background – is not recorded, but relations between the two were apparently initially cordial, with Howard praising the state of preparedness of Drake's squadron, and Sir Francis quickly convincing the lord admiral of the case for his offensive strategy. A few days after his arrival, Howard wrote to Lord Burghley of the privy council that he intended to sail for the coast of Spain as soon as possible: 'with intention to lie on and off betwixt England and that coast to watch the coming of the Spanish forces.' He had, however, guarded against any attempt by Parma to slip across the Channel by leaving Lord Henry Seymour with a forty-strong squadron to guard the Straits of Dover. Indeed, the lord admiral probably over-insured in this respect by giving Seymour at least two of the newest of the Queen's Ships, *Vanguard* and *Rainbow*, which would have been

An Elizabethan seaman. The dress of seamen in both fleets was probably similar.

of more use engaged against the Armada from the start of the campaign.

Howard's main worry was, and would remain, supplies. He found the Plymouth ships to be woefully under-provisioned. On 7 June, possibly indirectly criticising Drake, he told Burghley: 'I perceive that the ships and also the victuals be nothing in that readiness that I looked they should be in… We have here now about eighteen days' victuals and there is none to be gotten in all this county.' However, Howard had nothing but praise for his officers and men: 'There is here the gallantest company of captains, soldiers and mariners that I think ever was seen in England. It were a pity they should lack meat when they are so desirous to spend their lives in Her Majesty's service.'

Campaign Chronicle

The crews at Plymouth had already been on reduced rations, and by 15 June supplies were virtually exhausted, and the seamen had to subsist as best they could. It was not until 3 July that one month's supplies eventually arrived.

Howard was determined to waste no time before getting to sea, and as his men feverishly re-provisioned their ships through the night, he wrote to the queen: 'God willing, we will be under sail tomorrow morning.' With a fair wind, nearly 100 English ships put to sea out of Plymouth on the morning of 4 July. Within two days they were far out in the Bay of Biscay, bound for Corunna.

Hopes were running high that the Spaniards could be caught in port and comprehensively destroyed. Thomas Fenner of the *Nonpareil* exulted: 'There never happened the like opportunity to beat down the Spanish pride.' Then, with Corunna almost within reach, the wind dropped, leaving the English fleet becalmed for several days. When the breeze eventually freshened, it was blowing from the south, no longer favourable for the English, and indeed, raising the possibility that the Armada might slip past them undetected and reach the English coast first.

Howard had no option but to return to Plymouth, where frantic efforts began to resupply the squadron for the battle all felt to be imminent. Howard, who by now had developed a considerable pride in his ships and their crews, responded angrily to criticism of their condition on reaching Plymouth: 'I have heard that there is in London some hard speeches against Mr Hawkins because the *Hope* came in [to] mend a leak which she had. Sir, I think there were never so many of the prince's ships so long abroad, and in such seas, with such weather as these have had, with so few leaks; and the greatest fault of the *Hope* came with ill-grounding before our coming hither; and yet it is nothing to be spoken of. It was such a leak that I durst have gone with it to Venice.'

As tension mounted, efforts had continued to prepare England's defences on land. There were still fears that a 'fifth column' of English Catholics might stage an uprising in support of a landing by Parma. In fact, the vast majority of them –whatever their religious beliefs – had no desire to see England fall under Spain's control. However, as a precaution, the privy council ordered a number of leading English Catholics to be interned in Wisbeach Castle until the danger was over.

In an effort to whip up popular patriotic fervour, various government-inspired propaganda stories were circulated, retailing lurid tales of the horrors, tortures, and massacres planned by the Spaniards. Added to the anti-Catholic propaganda, which had been propagated for many years, these stories would, it was hoped, ensure that strongly Protestant areas, such as London, would fight desperately against the invader.

In fact, the evidence for ordinary folks' determination to fight was distinctly mixed. Even in Cornwall, seemingly one of the most threatened counties, where

20 June–23 July: Final Preparations

Men of the London Trained Bands. These were probably better dressed and equipped than many other such units.

6,000 militia were theoretically available, these were 'the roughest and most mutinous men in England, and during haytime and harvest, in particular, when the Armada was most likely to appear off the coast, perhaps as many as half might have refused to answer a call to arms.' Indeed, judging by their less than impressive performance a few years later, when a small Spanish galley force raided Penzance, it is debatable whether even those who had appeared would have put up serious resistance. In Kent, Parma's intended landing place, many people were said to be indifferent as to which side won.

Work was continuing on refurbishing and manning the chain of beacons intended to carry word of the Armada's sighting quickly to all parts of the kingdom. Many local communities, however, remained seemingly indifferent to the threat. Some inland areas were reluctant to provide financial contributions for the upkeep of military forces, and even in some of the most threatened localities, the quality of the militia who were available was extremely mixed. Sir George Carey, governor of the Isle of Wight, described the levies under his command as 'a band of men termed trained, who I find rather so in name than in deed.'

Campaign Chronicle

Despite efforts to re-equip them, many men of the trained bands were still armed with bows, including up to one-third of those in Surrey and Kent.

Work had also begun on constructing or refurbishing fortifications in vulnerable places. On the Isle of Wight, an entrenchment 8 feet wide and 4 feet high, manned by musketeers, was built with the rather optimistic hope that it would 'give some terror to the enemy on landing.' Carey also had a few guns mounted to cover likely landing spots, but he had only one day's supply of ammunition for them.

Given the Army of Flanders' well-attested ability to march up to ten miles a day, it is doubtful whether an effective force could have been concentrated after a Spanish landing in Kent to oppose Parma's advance on London. Sir Walter Ralegh was not the only experienced commander to believe the only chance of stopping the Spaniards was at sea.

The summer of 1588 was unusually stormy, which Lord Henry Seymour, commanding the English squadron in the Straits of Dover, felt might be of some benefit to Elizabeth's ships: 'Such summer season saw I never the like; for what for storms and variable unsettled winds, the same unsettleth and altereth our determinations for lying on the other coast, having of late sundry times put over, with southerly winds, so far as Calais; and suddenly enforced, still with westerly great gales, to return to our English coasts, where, so long as this unstable weather holdeth, and that same serveth well many times for the Spaniards to come, yet shall they be as greatly dangered by the raging seas as with their enemies.'

Medina Sidonia might have been encouraged had he known of enemy weaknesses. By the time he entered Corunna, the experience of the storm and his supply problems had evidently severely dampened his already ambivalent attitude towards his mission. Initially, after the flagship had entered harbour, and before the remainder of the fleet was scattered by the bad weather, the duke had appeared optimistic, telling the king that as soon as he had re-provisioned and the wind was in his favour, he would put to sea again: 'So I hope only to stay here for a short time.'

However, this seemingly positive view did not last for long. By 21 June, Medina Sidonia was reporting the effects of the sudden storm on the Armada: 'The people of the country say that so violent a sea and wind, accompanied by fog and tempest, have never been seen… Many men are falling sick, aided by the short commons and bad food, and I am afraid that this trouble may spread and become past remedy.'

Three days later, Medina Sidonia, possibly influenced by the views of experienced seamen like Juan Martinez de Recalde, was clearly despairing of the feasibility of the whole enterprise, risking the wrath of the king by suggesting the strength of the Armada was far too inadequate for the task required of it, and that it might be better instead to come to terms with the enemy. While he awaited Philip's reply, the duke called a council of war of those of his commanders who had so far reached Corunna, in order to consider his next move. He asked first whether the Armada should sail at once, without waiting for the twenty-eight ships that were still missing. As the men aboard these vessels made up something like one-third of the Armada's effective strength, the council, unsurprisingly, agreed it was better to wait. Don Francisco de Bobadilla, the duke's military adviser, was particularly adamant, feeling: 'If we go short-handed, the risk will be great, especially in the face of the forces we know the enemy now has. In case of misfortune to the Armada the Indies would be lost, and Portugal and Flanders in dire peril of being lost as well.'

Only Don Pedro de Valdez, commander of the Andalusian Squadron, while admitting to serious supply shortages, thought the Armada should sail at once. He was outvoted by the remainder of the council, and his attitude seems only to have incurred the displeasure of Medina Sidonia, probably influenced by his chief of staff, Diego Flores de Valdez, cousin and noted enemy of Don Pedro.

Perhaps surprisingly, while King Philip continued to press Medina Sidonia to sail as quickly as possible, his response to the duke's letter was fairly mild, retorting that 'if it [the Armada] were now to remain in Corunna, this would be construed as a proof of our weakness, and far from enhancing our prestige at the treaty negotiations (if, indeed, we were working to conclude a treaty) would provide the enemy with an opportunity to rise to greater heights of insolence.' It may, however, have been Medina Sidonia's obvious doubts that caused Philip not to pass on to him Parma's concerns regarding the feasibility of his making a rendezvous with the Armada.

By the middle of July, however, all of the stragglers had rejoined the Armada, and fresh food and water had done something to restore the health of its crews. It also apparently boosted Medina Sidonia's confidence, so that on 15 July he informed Philip that: 'With God's help, I hope to have everything ready for sailing tomorrow or the day after, weather permitting. I have already had the squadrons of Diego Flores, Valdez, Oquendo and Ojeda towed out of the harbour, and the rest will go outside tomorrow. We can then take advantage of the first fair wind to get clear away.'

Soon after 3.00 am on 23 July, the required south-easterly wind sprang up, and by that evening the whole Armada was at sea, bound at last for England.

And yet Medina Sidonia's concerns, as expressed in his letter to Philip, are worth quoting in detail:

'Your Majesty ordered me to go to Lisbon to fit out this armada and take charge of it. When I accepted the task I submitted to Your Majesty many reasons, in the interest of your service, why it was better that I should not do so. This was not because I wished to refuse the work, but because I recognised that we were attacking a kingdom so powerful, and so warmly aided by its neighbours, and that we should need a much larger force than Your Majesty had collected at Lisbon. This was my reason for at first declining the command, seeing that the enterprise was being represented to Your Majesty as easier than it was known to be by those whose only aim was Your Majesty's service.

'Nevertheless, matters reached a point when Your Majesty ordered me to sail, which I did, and we have now arrived at this port scattered and maltreated in such a way that we are much inferior in strength to the enemy... Many of our largest ships are still missing... whilst on the ships that are here there are many sick, whose numbers will increase in consequence of the bad provisions... By this Your Majesty may judge whether we can proceed on the voyage, upon the success of which so much depends...'

While Recalde, in a letter to the king dated 11 July, not only highlights Medina Sidonia's concerns about supplies, but also his own regarding a workable strategy:

'I have not been able to help [Medina Sidonia] much lately in consequence of an attack of sciatica, but thank God the remedies applied have been efficacious, and I rose today without pain. The duke came to see me yesterday and we discussed at length the sailing of the expedition. He seems to be much vexed at having to hurry the departure. I showed him how important speed was for the attainment of the object. He is in great fear that the stores and provisions which are being collected here will not be got together in time to supply the needs of the Armada. Profiting by the permission which Your Majesty... gave me... I will state my own opinion on the matter.

'So far as I understand, the object of the Armada is to meet and vanquish the enemy by main force, which I hope to God we shall do if he will fight us, and doubtless he will.

'In the contrary case we have to proceed to the Downs [a large sheltered anchorage off the English coast between Dover and Margate], and there join hands with the Duke of Parma's force in Dunkirk, whose passage across we are to protect to the most convenient point which may be agreed upon. This point should be the nearest possible one on either side of the Thames.

'This will take some little time, as in the case of there being a cavalry force, as I understand there will be, it cannot be carried over in one passage, and we shall be fortunate if it can be done in two.

'After this be done, the first thing will be to obtain a port for the Armada. If it be found possible to obtain anchorage and shelter in the river itself, supported by the army, no further reinforcements will be needed; or at least those from Flanders will suffice. I imagine from what I can see, however, that Flanders will be much exhausted, and the help from there inconsiderable. From the mouth of the Thames to Southampton – about 40 leagues – I know of no port capable of taking large vessels, all the coast being very uninviting. The harbours of Southampton and the Isle of Wight are well defended by forts, and it appears to me that the most convenient and easiest ports for landing would be Falmouth, Plymouth or Dartmouth, especially as the highly necessary reinforcements of men and stores will have to be sent from Spain, and isolated vessels will be exposed to much danger from the enemy higher up the Channel.

'I see, nevertheless, the objection to separating the Armada from the land force. Of the two difficulties I do not presume to judge which is the lesser.

'In the case of our encountering and defeating the enemy, I feel sure that he will not suffer so much damage as to be unable to repair, at all events sufficiently to impede, the passage of our reinforcements high up the Channel. But it will be difficult for him to do this if our armada be stationed in the above-mentioned ports, lying nearest to Spain. If it be possible for the reinforcement to be sent in strength sufficient to attack these ports, whilst the conquest is being effected higher up, that will be the best course. In that case, after the Army of Flanders had been taken across and strengthened, the Armada might return towards Ushant and meet the reinforcements with which it might enter one of the said ports, and then either push a force inland towards the Bristol Channel, or form a junction with the other army.'

In comparison, Howard's main concern was neither provisions nor strategy, but reliable intelligence, as shown in his report to Walsingham:

'I am sure you have seen the letter which I sent unto Her Majesty, of the discovery of certain of the Spanish fleet not far off Scilly, which made me make as much haste out to sea as I could; for upon Sunday our victuals came to us, and having the wind at the north-east, I would not stay in the taking in of them all; but taking in some part of them, I appointed the rest to follow with me, and so bore to Scilly, thinking to have cut off those Spanish ships seen there, from the rest of their fleet; but the wind continued not sixteen hours there, but turned south-south-west, that we were fain to lie off and on in the Sleeve [Western Approaches at the entrance to the Channel], and could go no further.

'Then did I send Sir Francis Drake, with half a score ships and three or four pinnaces, to discover. In his way, hard about Ushant, he met with a man of mine, whom I had sent in a bark, ten days before to lie off and on there for discovery, who had met with an Irish bark, and staid her, which had been on the 22nd taken by eighteen great ships of the Spanish fleet, 16 leagues south-south-west of Scilly. They had taken out of the said bark five of her most principal men, and left in her but three men and a boy. One of the greatest Spanish ships towed her at her stern by a cable, which in the night time, the wind blowing somewhat stiff, broke, and so she escaped in the storm. This did assure us greatly that the Spanish fleet was broken in the storm afore; and by all likelihood, we conjectured, if the wind had continued northerly, that they would have returned again for the Groyne [Corunna]; but [as] the wind hath served these six or seven days, [we] must look for them every hour if they mean to come hither.

'Sir, I sent a fine Spanish *caravel* [a small, fast sailing ship] on, eight days agone, to the Groyne to learn intelligence, such a one as would not have been mistrusted; but when she was 50 leagues on her way, this southerly wind forced her back again unto us. Therefore I pray you, if you hear or understand of any news or advertisement by land, that I may hear of them from you with expedition.

'I have divided myself here into three parts, and yet we lie within sight of one another; so as if any of us do discover the Spanish fleet, we give notice thereof presently the one to another, and thereupon repair and assemble together. I myself lie towards Ushant; and Mr Hawkins, with as many more, lieth towards Scilly. Thus are we fain to do; or else, with this wind, they might pass by, and we never the wiser. Whatsoever had been made of the Sleeve, it is another manner of thing than it was taken for. We find it by experience, and daily observation, to be 100 miles over: a large room for me to look unto …'

23–30 July 1588: Enemy in Sight

By 26 July the Armada, heading northwards, was out of sight of land, and the breeze, hitherto very light, began to freshen. This was rapidly followed by stormy weather and rain squalls, which forced the Spaniards – whose primitive navigational aids and charts could provide only an approximation of their position – further west to gain sea-room. Early victims of the storm were Admiral Medrano's four galleys. Medina Sidonia knew the potential value of the

Elizabethan artillery in action. The Armada carried a number of heavy siege guns, some of which appear to have been employed on board ships.

galleys in guarding Parma's force against attack, and in supporting his landing, and urged Medrano to make every effort to continue: 'I sent two *pataches* [pinnaces] to stand by the galleys in case they should require assistance, and all that day the three galleys were in sight. But after nightfall, when the weather became thick with very heavy rain, they were lost sight of, and we have never seen them more... Not only did the waves mount to the skies, but some seas broke clean over the ships... It was the most cruel night ever seen.'

In fact all four of the galleys managed to reach the coast of France in the vicinity of Bordeaux, although one of them, the *Diana*, was so badly damaged as to be beached and never put to sea again.

An equally serious and more mysterious casualty was the carrack *Santa Ana* of Recalde's Biscayan Squadron. There had been earlier problems with this ship, which after the Armada had been scattered by gales off Corunna, had eventually fetched up in her home port of Santander, instead of obeying instructions and making for Corunna. Whether this was a result of disaffection among her crew never became clear, but she now once again parted company with the Armada, and headed off half way up the Channel and entered the French port of Le Havre, never to rejoin the fleet.

So, even before he encountered the English fleet, Medina Sidonia had lost five valuable fighting ships. It is sometimes claimed that the Spanish crews were unused to coping with such stormy conditions. But in fact most of the seamen had considerable experience of voyages in the Atlantic and the West Indies, although many of the Mediterranean crewmen in the galleys and the Levanters, like Medina Sidonia himself, would not have had experience of Atlantic gales.

In many cases, the high superstructure of the Spanish ships made them more susceptible to these rough conditions than was the case with their 'race-built' English counterparts. The storm was described by the log of one Spanish vessel in awed terms: 'The sea so high that that all the mariners said they had never seen the like in July.' John Hawkins, who was caught on the fringes of the same storm as he returned to Plymouth, dismissed it as a 'little flaw'.

When dawn broke on 26 July, Medina Sidonia found that forty of his ships had parted company during the gale. His pinnaces were despatched to round them up, and bring them to the agreed rendezvous off the Scilly Isles, which Medina Sidonia himself reached on the 29th. But it was late on the following morning (Saturday, 30 July) before the last of the stragglers rejoined, among them the *capitana* (flagship) of the galleasses, *San Lorenzo*, whose rudder had been damaged. Medina Sidonia observed gloomily: 'These craft are really very fragile for heavy seas.'

At 4.00 pm on the previous day, lookouts in the tops of the flagship, *San Martin*, had caught their first glimpse of England, as the crags of the rocky Lizard Peninsula loomed dimly on the horizon. Medina Sidonia responded to the sight of enemy land by ordering the Holy Banner to be hoisted at his masthead, together with his battle flag, a huge banner bearing a device of Christ Crucified with the Virgin Mary and Mary Magdalene on its reverse. Other ships followed suit, displaying a colourful array of their provincial flags and the personal banners of their commanders and the nobility who were on-board.

It may have been dawn on the 30th before the Spaniards were sighted by their opponents. On the Lizard, and in a lengthening chain to the east, the smoke of warning beacons could be seen by the watching men in the Armada, while ashore the clamour of church bells called the Cornish militia to arms.

The first sighting of the Armada at sea was by Captain Thomas Fleming's bark (a small sailing ship), *Golden Hind*, one of a line of small craft deployed by Howard to the west of Plymouth to provide warning of the enemy's approach. Early on the afternoon of the 30th, Fleming entered Plymouth Sound to bring word that the Armada had arrived.

What happened next is the stuff of one of the best-known stories of popular English history. Howard and his commanders were reportedly playing bowls on Plymouth Hoe when the news reached them. Drake was supposedly the first to respond, with the comment: 'We have time to finish the game and beat the Spaniards too.'

The earliest report of this incident comes some forty years later, and of Drake's words not until the eighteenth century, and doubts have been cast on their authenticity. In fact, there was good reason for Drake to have uttered these words, or something similar.

When Fleming reached Plymouth, the tide was in full flood, and Drake will have known there was no way in which the English fleet could clear the Sound and get out to sea in the face of a current running at 1 knot. The tide would not slacken until the evening, when the ebb set in, and only then would it be possible for the fleet to begin leaving harbour. So for the next few hours, once they had no doubt ordered all final preparations for battle to be made and alerted the shore defences, there was nothing the English commanders could do but wait – and they might well have 'finished the game'.

The great fear that must have been lurking in many minds was that the Spaniards might take advantage of the flood tide to attempt to enter the Sound and destroy the English fleet while it lay virtually helpless at anchor. It would in many ways have seemed an attractive course of action for Medina Sidonia, and Recalde, at least, had hinted at the desirability of such a move in his letter to the king. The duke himself was evidently uneasy about the king's insistence that he should if possible avoid battle with the enemy until after he had joined Parma.

But one clause in Philip's instructions read: 'If they are divided, it will be well to proceed to overcome them so they cannot all join forces.' This could be interpreted as permitting an attack on that part of the English fleet in Plymouth harbour. Certainly the situation on the morning of 30 July seemed to offer the best chance of such an attack, and Medina Sidonia called a council of war to consider his next move.

The discussion was evidently heated, with the duke and his commanders divided. The most aggressive and experienced of the Spanish commanders, Recalde, Oquendo, and Alonso de Leiva (secretly nominated by the king as Medina Sidonia's successor in case of need), favoured an attack on Plymouth, probably by landing troops to subdue the English batteries before the fighting ships entered the Sound. Medina Sidonia, however, was against an attack, citing the king's instructions and fearing heavy losses among his ships and men at the very start of the campaign.

In the end, a final decision was postponed until more information was available. The redoubtable Ensign Gill was sent in a small oared craft to gain intelligence. In the meantime, in thickening weather, the Armada continued slowly eastwards, sighting some sails, whose identity in the poor visibility could not be established.

Campaign Chronicle

In reality, there was probably no chance of the Spaniards being able to take the English fleet unawares in Plymouth. The Armada was too far away on 30 July to be able to enter the harbour with that afternoon's flood tide, and would have had no other opportunity until the following afternoon. In the event, the issue was decided when Ensign Gill returned that night with four captured Falmouth fishermen, who reported that they had seen Howard's fleet being towed out of harbour.

The news was a serious disappointment to Medina Sidonia, who had believed Howard and the bulk of the English fleet to be 250 miles away in the Straits of Dover, with only a small squadron under Drake in Plymouth. Until the situation clarified, he ordered the Armada to continue eastwards under shortened sail. But with the wind veering to the south-south-west, Diego Flores warned the duke that he risked getting ahead of the English fleet, so losing the advantage of the weather-gauge. Medina Sidonia ordered the Spanish fleet to anchor, in order to await what the dawn might bring.

Throughout the evening of 30 July Plymouth harbour had been the scene of feverish activity. With the ebb tide, though virtually no wind, Howard's men began to tow and warp (i.e., use fixed cables to winch the ships) their vessels out of harbour, and anchored in the lee (shelter) of Rame Head, where they waited for the morning ebb tide, due at about 11.00 am. With the aid of this and the south-south-westerly wind which had sprung up they were able – with a display of excellent seamanship – to beat clear of the Sound and begin to edge westwards, in order to get astern of the Armada and rob the Spaniards of the weather-gauge.

Medina Sidonia described the early stages of the Armada's voyage to King Philip:

'On 22 July 1588 the duke and the whole of the Armada sailed from Corunna with a SW wind, which continued for the next few days, the voyage being prosperous.

'On the 25th the duke sent Captain Don Rodrigo Tello to Dunkirk to advise the Duke of Parma of his coming, and to bring back intelligence of Parma's condition, and instructions with regard to the place where a junction of the forces should be effected.

'On the 26th the weather was dead calm and overcast, which lasted until midday. The wind then went round to the N. and the Armada sailed in an easterly direction until midnight, when the wind shifted to the WNW, with heavy rain-squalls. The leading galley *Diana* was missed this day. She was making so much water that the captain decided to run for a port.

'On the 27th the same wind blew, but fresher, with very heavy sea. This lasted until midnight, and the storm caused a large number of ships and the other three galleys to separate from the Armada.

'On Thursday, the 28th, the day broke clear and sunny, the wind and sea being more moderate. At dawn there were forty ships and the three galleys missing, whereupon the duke ordered the lead to be cast, and bottom was found at 75 fathoms, 75 leagues from the Scillies. The duke then despatched three *pataches*: one to the Lizard to see if the missing ships were there, and order them to await the Armada; another to reconnoitre the land; and a third to return on the course by which we have come to order the ships to make more sail, and bring up stragglers.

'On Friday, the 29th, the Armada continued sailing with a westerly wind. The *patache* that went to the Lizard brought back news that our missing ships were ahead, under Don Pedro de Valdez, who had collected them and was awaiting the Armada. During the afternoon all the ships, except Juan Martinez' flagship, with Maestre de Campo Nicolas de Isla on-board, and the three galleys joined the Armada. The English coast was first sighted on this day. It was said to be Cape Lizard.

'On the 30th, at dawn, the Armada was very near the shore. We were seen by the people on land, who made signal fires, and in the afternoon the duke sent Ensign Juan Gill in a rowing boat to obtain intelligence. In the afternoon of the same day a number of ships were sighted, but as the weather was thick and rainy they could not be counted. Ensign Gill returned at night with four fishermen in a boat, hailing, as they said, from Falmouth. They reported that they had seen the English fleet leave Plymouth that afternoon under the lord admiral of England, and Drake.'

Admiral Lord Howard related the opening moves by the English fleet:

'The 19 July [29th NS] we had intelligence by one of the barks that his lordship had left in the Sleeve for discovery… wherein was Captain Thomas Fleming, that the fleet of Spain was seen near the Lizard, the wind then being southerly or south-west; and although the greater number of ships of the English army, being then in Plymouth, with that wind was very hard to be gotten out of harbour, yet the same was done with such diligence and good will, that many of them got abroad as though it had been with a fair wind. Whereupon on the 20th July [30th NS], his lordship, with fifty-four sail of his fleet, with that south-west wind plied out of the Sound; and being gotten out scarce as far as Eddystone the Spanish army was discovered, and were apparently seen of the whole fleet to the westwards as far as Fowey.'

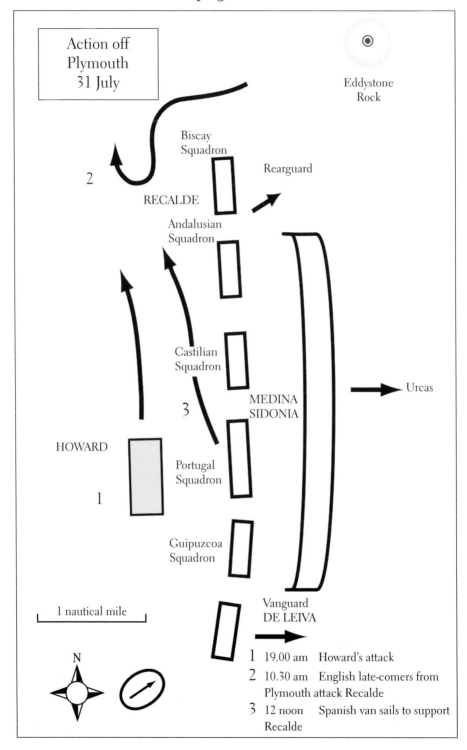

Action off
Plymouth
31 July

2

Biscay
Squadron

RECALDE

Eddystone
Rock

Rearguard

Andalusian
Squadron

Urcas

Castilian
Squadron

3

MEDINA
SIDONIA

HOWARD

Portugal
Squadron

1

Guipuzcoa
Squadron

1 nautical mile

Vanguard
DE LEIVA

N

1   19.00 am   Howard's attack
2   10.30 am   English late-comers from
             Plymouth attack Recalde
3   12 noon   Spanish van sails to support
             Recalde

Sunday 31 July, 9.00 am–1.00 pm: First Blood – the Fleets Clash off Plymouth

Wind and Weather: wind WNW, rising; sea becoming rough

As the early morning mists cleared, Medina Sidonia saw the unwelcome sight of at least eighty-five English ships to windward of him, about 5 miles to the west of the Eddystone Rock. Other English ships, late departures from Plymouth, formed a straggling line to the north, between the Armada and the Cornish coast to within about 2 miles of the fishing village of Looe.

The Spanish commanders were probably shaken by this display of English seamanship. It had given Howard the all-important advantage of the weather-gauge, and meant that his fleet could follow their intended strategy of 'coursing' (harrying) the Armada up-Channel, harassing any Spanish attempt to make a landing on the English coast. Not only had the English fleet gained a vital tactical advantage by gaining the windward side of the Armada, but any lingering thoughts Medina Sidonia may have had of trapping Howard within the confines of Plymouth Sound were finally dashed.

Howard's plan seems to have been for the ships under his own command to maintain pressure on the centre of the Spanish formation, while Drake's and Hawkins' squadrons attacked the potentially vulnerable tips of the horns of the *lunula*.

The Ark Royal.

The Lunula

This was the famous crescent-like formation adopted by the Armada during most of the campaign in the Channel. It was not a new development, being the favoured formation of a number of Spanish and Italian naval theorists, and had already been decided upon before the Armada sailed. All but the smallest ships had a place in the formation. The *lunula* consisted of the main body, or *battalia*, in the centre, and two wings or horns: the *cuerno derecho* on the right, and the *cuerno aquierado* on the left. The most powerful fighting ships were distributed between the *battalia* and the *cuernos*, with two smaller reserve bodies, known as *soccoros*, supporting each wing. The *lunula* proved very effective for its purpose of enabling the Armada to hold off English attacks while continuing its voyage up-Channel. Howard's fleet never succeeded in breaking its formation in battle.

The English were overawed by their first sight of the mighty Armada. Henry Whyte, captain of the 200-ton *Bark Talbot*, admitted even to the formidable Sir Francis Walsingham that: 'The majesty of the enemy's fleet, the good order they held, and the private consideration of our own wards, did cause, in my opinion, our first onset to be more coldly done than became the valour of our nation and the credit of the English navy.'

As the English fleet approached to contact, Howard, in a chivalrous gesture that was probably entirely lost on hard-bitten privateers like Drake and Frobisher, sent the pinnace *Disdain* darting forward to fire a challenging shot at what he believed to be the Spanish flagship, but seems actually to have been de Leiva's *La Rata Santa Maria Encoronada*. In any case, the symbolic action was hardly needed: both sides knew by 9.00 am that battle was imminent.

Spanish eyewitnesses described Howard's attack on the centre and rear of the Armada as being made *en ala* ('in file'), which has led to suggestions by some writers that the English fleet was formed in 'line of battle', similar to that employed by fleets at the height of the Age of Sail. This seems unlikely, as such a formation was apparently not part of recognised English tactics until almost a century later. Howard's ships most probably made their attack in a rough echelon formation, firing their particularly heavy bow chasers as they approached, then, in a rough figure-of-eight manoeuvre, turn to fire a broadside, then their stern guns, and finally their second broadside, before retiring to reload.

The weight of Howard's initial attack fell on de Leiva's *Rata*, while Drake was heading for Recalde's rearguard, forming the northern wing of the Armada, which could still conceivably threaten Plymouth. While the straggling English

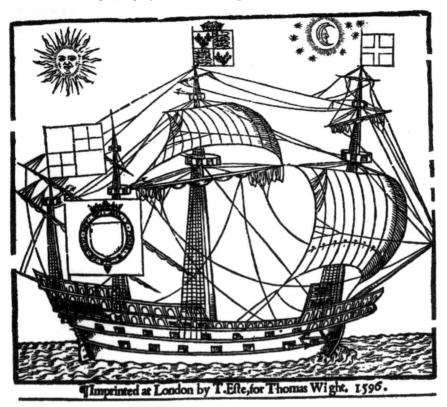

An older ship of the 'Navy Royal', possibly the Triumph.

ships still coming out of Plymouth harassed the landward wing of the Armada, Howard, after his initial engagement with the Spanish centre, seems to have moved northwards to support Drake, who had about forty ships, firing as he did so at a long-range of over 400 yards.

The impact of Drake's first assault, made by his strongest ships, which included his own *Revenge* and two other large Queen's Ships, *Victory* and *Triumph*, apparently caused some panic among the *naos* of Recalde's Biscayan Squadron, which veered away from the attackers towards the centre of the Armada, resulting in some confusion: while Recalde himself, who had shortened sail and turned his *San Juan de Portugal* broadside on to the attackers in order to bring his guns to bear, found himself temporarily alone.

Seeing Recalde under heavy fire, Medina Sidonia ordered part of his van, under de Leiva, from the unengaged right horn of the Armada, to go to the support of the *San Juan*, which had meanwhile been belatedly joined by Recalde's *almirante* (second in command), the *Gran Grin*. De Leiva brought with him the

Portuguese galleon *San Mateo*, two other galleons, and Hugo de Moncada's four galleasses, which the English were seeing in action for the first time.

If, has been suggested, Recalde had deliberately acted as bait in order to draw Drake's squadron to close quarters, he and de Leiva were quickly disappointed. Drake declined to fall into the trap, and pulled back, though continuing to direct an intense fire at the 1,050-ton *San Juan* at a range of 300 to 400 yards.

The duel continued indecisively for two hours until about 1.00 pm, with Howard providing some support for Drake. By this time, further Spanish ships, including Medina Sidonia's *San Martin*, and Pedro de Valdez' *socorro* (battlegroup) were also heading for the scene of action, and the battered *San Juan* was able to pull back into the centre of the Armada for hasty repairs. An infantry officer, Pedro Estrade, aboard the galleon *San Marcos*, suggests the galleasses were quick to make an impact on their opponents: 'The vice admiral of the galleasses went putting himself into our horn of Don Pedro de Valdez, and the English, when they saw the galleasses to enter, they retired, and went away all that they could.'

As Medina Sidonia lowered his topsails in an invitation to fight, the English fleet pulled back out of range and ceased fire. The first action of the campaign was over, and as the Armada prepared to resume its formation and continue eastwards up-Channel, it was time for the opposing commanders to assess its results.

Medina Sidonia described the engagement to King Philip:

'On Sunday, the 31st, the day broke with the wind changed to the WNW in Plymouth Roads, and eighty ships were sighted to windward of us; and towards the coast to leeward eleven other ships were seen, including three large galleons which were cannonading some of our vessels. They gradually got to windward and joined their own fleet.

'Our armada placed itself in fighting order, the flagship hoisting the royal standard at the foremast. The enemy's fleet passed, cannonading our vanguard, which was under Don Alonso de Leiva, and then fell on the rearguard commanded by Admiral Juan Martinez de Recalde. The latter, in order to keep his place and repel the attack, although he saw his rearguard was leaving him unsupported and joining the rest of the Armada, determined to await the fight. The enemy attacked him so fiercely with cannon that they crippled his rigging, breaking his stay, and striking his foremast twice with cannon balls. He was supported by the *Gran Grin*, a ship of the rearguard, and others, The royal flagship then struck her foresail, slackened her sheets, and lay to until Recalde joined the main squadron, when the enemy sheered off, and the duke collected his fleet.'

31 July, 9.00 am–1.00 pm: First Blood

A Spanish officer, Pedro de Calderon, aboard the hulk (storeship) *San Salvador*, had a close view of the engagement between de Leiva's force and Drake's squadron, noting that the English 'flagship':

'Struck her foresail, and from the direction of the land sent four vessels, one of which was the vice-flagship to skirmish with our vice-flagship [Recalde] and the rest of our rearguard. They bombarded her and the galleon *San Mateo*, which, putting her head as close up to the wind as possible, did not reply to their fire, but waited for them in the hope of bringing them to close quarters. The *Rata*, with Don Alonso de Leiva on-board, endeavoured to approach the enemy's vice-flagship [the *Revenge*], which allowed herself to fall towards the *Rata*. But they would not exchange cannon shots, because the enemy's ship, fearing that the *San Mateo* would bring her to close quarters, left the 'Rata' and bombarded the *San Mateo*. Meanwhile, the wind forced Don Alonso de Leiva away, and he was prevented from carrying out his intentions, but he exchanged cannon shots with other enemy ships. Juan Martinez de Recalde, like the skilful seaman he was, collected all his ships whilst protecting his rearguard, engaging at the same time eight of the enemy's best ships. The duke's flagship most distinguished herself this day, as she was engaged the greater part of the time, and resisted the fury of the whole of the enemy's fleet.'

Lord Howard and Drake were both terse in their initial comments. Howard wrote to Sir Francis Walsingham that:

'At nine of the clock we gave them fight, which continued until one… We made some of them bear room to stop their leaks, not withstanding we durst not adventure to put in amongst them, their fleet being so strong.'

Drake cautiously told Lord Henry Seymour, anxiously awaiting news in the Straits of Dover:

'The 21st [31st NS] we had them in chase, and so, coming up to them, there hath passed some cannon shot between some of our fleet and some of them, and as far as we perceive, they are determined to sell their lives with blows.'

In August, writing, at rather more leisure, his official account to the privy council, Howard puts a rather more positive slant on the engagement:

'The next morning, being Sunday, 21 July 1588 [31st NS], all the English ships that there were then come out of Plymouth had recovered the wind off Eddystone, and about nine of the clock in the morning, the lord admiral sent his pinnace, named *Disdain*, to give the Duke of Medina defiance, and afterward in the *Ark* bear up with the admiral of the Spaniards, wherein the duke was supposed to be, and fought with her till she was rescued by divers ships of the Spanish army. In the meantime, Sir Francis Drake, Sir John Hawkins and Sir Martin Frobisher fought with the galleon of Portugal, wherein John Martinez de Recalde, vice admiral, was supposed to be. The fight was so well maintained for the time that the enemy was constrained to give way and bear up room to the eastward.'

Reviewing the course of their first encounter, neither commander had grounds for total satisfaction. The English fleet had fired off a great deal of powder and shot, so much, indeed, that Howard was already calling urgently for new supplies. But firing at too long a range, they had done little harm to the Spaniards. Recalde, for example, had lost only fifteen men aboard his *San Juan*, which had suffered quite minor damage. As the experienced seaman Richard Hawkins once observed: 'How much the nearer, so much the better, he that shooteth far off at sea had as good as not shoot at all.' Howard and his commanders also had grounds for concern at their failure to break up the Armada's formation, apart from an initial panic in Recalde's squadron.

On the credit side, however, Howard could comfort himself with the knowledge that, if Medina Sidonia had ever intended to enter Plymouth, the morning's fighting had carried the Armada too far east for that now to be possible. And the English retained the all-important weather-gauge.

The aspect of the enemy that had forcibly impressed itself on the Spaniards in that first encounter had been the speed and manoeuvrability of the English ships. Moving sometimes three or four times faster than their opponents, the English galleons were proving infuriatingly adept at thwarting Spanish attempts to close and board them. However, despite concern about the discipline and commitment of some of his captains, Medina Sidonia could take satisfaction in the failure of the English to penetrate his formation, or seriously damage any of his ships, despite what was obviously a much faster firing rate. He would, however, shortly have much more serious grounds for concern.

Sunday 31 July, 1.00 pm–c. Midnight: Setbacks for the Spaniards
Wind and Weather: wind WNW; seas remain rough
As the fighting died down, the ships of the Armada began to return to their original positions in the *lunula*. Soon after 1.00 pm Don Pedro de Valdez's 1,150-

ton flagship of the Andalusian Squadron, *Nuestra Senõra del Rosario*, collided with one of Recalde's Biscayans, damaging her bowsprit, and affecting her steering ability. Attempts at repairs had only just begun when, at about 4.00 pm, the Spaniards heard the sound of a huge explosion.

The victim was the 850-ton Guipuzcoan *San Salvador*, which, as well as being one of the most heavily armed ships in the Armada, carried its paymaster and much of the money intended to pay the crews. As the clouds of smoke cleared, it could be seen that the stern castle of the *San Salvador*, together with her steering, had been badly damaged, with her two highest after-decks completely blown out. Over 200 of her crew had been killed.

Medina Sidonia brought the Armada to a halt while successful efforts were made to bring the fire under control. Boats were sent to ferry the *San Salvador*'s treasure to other ships, along with most of her injured. Rumours were soon sweeping the Armada regarding the cause of the explosion. The most likely explanation – an accident with gunpowder – was the least popular. More lurid reports suggested the blast had been the work of a disaffected German gunner, either after he had been reprimanded by a Spanish officer or in revenge for an attack on his wife, who had evaded the order against women sailing with the Armada, and remained on-board. A little support for this latter theory is perhaps provided by an English report that a German woman was among the survivors later taken from the ship.

No sooner had *San Salvador* been taken in tow and pulled back to the safety of the main body of the Armada, than another disaster occurred. The steadily rising seas were making it increasingly difficult for the damaged *Rosario* to steer properly. Soon after 4.00 pm she suffered another collision, this time with fellow Andalusian *Santa Catalina*. *Rosario*'s foremast and yard were brought down, falling on her mainmast and rendering Pedro de Valdez' ship unmanageable.

De Valdez sent a message to Medina Sidonia asking for assistance. However, according to one version of events, Medina Sidonia's chief of staff, Diego Flores de Valdez (Pedro's cousin), tried to dissuade the duke from halting the Armada again in order to assist the *Rosario*, saying that such an action would endanger the whole expedition. Strictly speaking, he was probably correct, although there were plausible suggestions that Diego's advice was influenced by the known enmity between him and his cousin.

Medina Sidonia, however, disregarded the advice, and a number of ships, including the galleon *San Francisco* and Medina Sidonia's own *San Martin* clustered around the stricken *Rosario*. In a rather surprising move, Medina Sidonia passed a tow line from his own ship to *Rosario*, but the rope parted in the rising seas, and it proved impossible to pass another one. With evident reluctance, the duke now heeded his chief of staff's advice, and after Don Pedro had declined an offer to come on-board the flagship, the Armada resumed its course, leaving four pinnaces to watch the crippled *Rosario* as she wallowed helplessly behind.

On-board the galleon *San Mateo*, Pedro Estrade witnessed the abandoning of the *Rosario*: 'Then again she fires off four pieces, but there were none that came to succour her, for that the wind did blow much, the sea was grown, and the English did follow us. At prayer time we left her, for that the Duke of Medina did shoot off a piece with a bullet by which we proceeded on our way. After, we understood that she was boarded with five galleons, who did much harm unto Don Pedro and slew all his people.'

While there can be no doubt the abandonment of the *Rosario* was the correct course of action from the viewpoint of the Armada's mission, Medina Sidonia's action caused deep concern throughout the fleet, as other captains assumed that in similar circumstances they too would be left to their fate. It was the opinion of more than one Spaniard that morale in the Armada never recovered from this setback.

For the moment, however, Medina Sidonia had more pressing concerns. He was becoming increasingly worried at having received no news from the Duke of Parma, and that evening sent off a pinnace commanded by Ensign Juan Gill to run the gauntlet of Seymour and the Dutch, and acquaint Parma with events. He also begged that Parma should despatch him some pilots familiar with the Flemish coast, in case bad weather should force him to seek refuge there:

'Two Leagues off Plymouth 31 July 1588

'I intend with God's help to continue on my voyage without letting anything divert me, until I receive instructions from your Excellency of what I am to do and where I am to wait for you to join me. I implore your Excellency to send someone who with the utmost speed, bringing replies to the points on which I have written to you, also to send me pilots for the coast of Flanders, for without them I am ignorant of the places where I can find shelter in ships as large as these in case I should be overtaken by the slightest storm.

'P.S. The enemy continue to harass our rear and… their ships now seem to have increased to over 100 sail: some are excellent vessels, and all of them very fast sailers. Their ships are so fast and nimble, they can do anything they like with them.'

As darkness fell, Medina Sidonia – declining food other than bread and cheese – continued to pace the deck of his flagship, a prey to increasing anxiety.

At about the same time, Howard called a council of war aboard *Ark Royal*. The English commanders were agreed that on balance they had had the better of the first day of fighting. They had prevented any attack on Plymouth, but it was becoming clear, despite the problems in the Armada they had witnessed that afternoon, their gunnery had so far had no decisive effect on the enemy. Even Recalde's *San Juan*, which had been subjected to several hours' concentrated attack, had only suffered minor damage, and was now back on station with the Biscayans. Nor, despite momentary confusion, had the English attacks succeeded in disrupting the Spanish formation. It seems that some of those present – probably in order to conserve ammunition – wanted to avoid further engagements until after they linked up with Seymour's squadron. We cannot know for sure who proposed this course of action: but in view of his comments – recorded in a letter penned to Walsingham that day – Howard himself seems a possibility. But the vote to carry on attacking the Armada 'was with difficulty carried upon the affirmative, especially by the sound and resolute arguments of Martin Frobisher'.

It was with mixed feelings, therefore, that the council of war broke up. Although there was a strong suspicion the Spaniards would attempt to seize the Isle of Wight, as the only sheltered anchorage available for them before they reached the Straits of Dover, the only way this danger could be securely countered was by overtaking the Spaniards and blocking their path. But this would lose Howard's fleet the vital advantage of the weather-gauge, and was clearly too great a risk to take.

Instead, it was agreed the English fleet would continue to follow the Armada during the night. Drake was appointed to lead the fleet, in *Revenge*, illuminating his stern lantern to serve as a guide.

All seemed to be going according to plan, when, around midnight, Drake's guiding light suddenly disappeared…

Monday 1 August: Drake Captures the *Rosario*

Wind and Weather: westerly wind, probably light to moderate; sea becomes calm by nightfall
During the night, due to the disappearance of Drake's guiding light, the English fleet had become scattered. Dawn, however, brought a rude shock for Lord Admiral Howard, who, with his own *Ark Royal*, and two other Queen's Ships, *Bear* and *Mary Rose*, realised that the stern lantern he had resumed following – in the belief that it was Drake's – actually belonged to a Spanish ship, and he was now in serious danger of running full tilt into the Armada.

There seemed, for a moment, an excellent opportunity for the Spaniards to score a major success. Hugh de Moncada saw an ideal situation to use his galleasses, and asked Medina Sidonia for permission to engage Howard: but 'this liberty the duke thought not good to permit unto him.' It is unclear whether the refusal was due to Medina Sidonia's view that the honour of engaging the

Campaign Chronicle

The capture of the Rosario.

English flagship should rest with him, or whether he had in mind King Philip's instructions to avoid battle whenever possible. Moncada, himself a man of prickly honour, was evidently deeply offended by the perceived rebuff.

In any event, the opportunity was fleeting. Howard and his consorts quickly put about and rejoined another portion of the English fleet, which happily came into view.

Howard was no doubt considerably agitated by Drake's absence, and his temper may not have been improved shortly afterwards, when – with the English fleet still helplessly scattered, precluding any action that day – a report of Drake's nocturnal activities arrived. A pinnace appeared, carrying Drake's account of how, soon after midnight, Sir Francis had sighted strange sails to starboard. Fearing, he claimed, that it might be a Spanish squadron trying to slip behind the English fleet and gain the weather-gauge, Drake doused his stern lantern – in order, he claimed, not to confuse the rest of the English fleet – and went in pursuit, with only his own *Revenge*, and Captain Jacob Whiddon's 300-ton Dartmouth privateer, *Roebuck*.

Discovering that the mystery ships were actually harmless German merchant-men, Drake reversed course to rejoin Howard, only to find himself, as dawn broke, within sight of nothing less than Pedro de Valdez's *Rosario*. De Valdez had already had an encounter during the night with another small English ship, the *Margaret and John*, which having skirmished inconclusively, rejoined the English fleet. Rather surprisingly, although apparently now abandoned by his escorting pinnaces, Don Pedro seems to have made no effort to carry out emergency repairs.

1 August: Drake Captures the *Rosario*

Sir Francis Drake: another portrait, but still with the world at his fingertips.

Drake hailed the *Rosario*, calling upon De Valdez to surrender or fight. After fairly prolonged parleying, De Valdez – already made furious by being abandoned by the rest of the Armada – on discovering his challenger to be none other than the celebrated Sir Francis Drake, agreed to yield to one 'whose valour and felicity was so great that Mars and Neptune seemed to attend him.' Don Pedro was granted full honours of war, and he and forty of his officers were taken aboard *Revenge*, where they were entertained in style, and watched the remainder of the campaign from the deck of Drake's flagship and the *Ark Royal*. His crew were less fortunate. *Rosario* was towed into Dartmouth by Captain Whiddon and stripped of her guns and ammunition: the latter being a welcome addition to Howard's dwindling supplies. Her crew were sent to rot in English prisons, where many died.

We do not know the nature of Drake's reception by Howard when he eventually hove into view, although it may be significant that the two men thereafter seem to have disliked each other. The lord admiral probably thought it impolitic to dismiss or court martial his most famous officer in the middle of a campaign, even though he was certainly guilty of disobedience and possibly dereliction of duty. It was equally difficult to discipline England's most popular hero when he had just gained such a major success. Howard seems to have decided that, on balance, it was best to accept Drake's version of events tacitly, and regard the matter as closed.

There, were, however, several puzzling aspects: not least, the amount of valuables aboard *Rosario*, which was declared by both Drake and Don Pedro to be considerably less than official Spanish records claimed. The possibility of their having struck a 'deal' to divide part of the spoils between them cannot be ruled out, and many contemporaries had little doubt that Sir Francis had allowed his privateering instincts to get the better of him, imperilling the English fleet in the process.

Chief among Drake's critics was Martin Frobisher, apparently for not entirely altruistic reasons. He commented later that Sir Francis: 'Like a coward kept by her [the *Rosario*] all night, because he would have the spoil. He thinketh to cozen us out of our share of 15,000 ducats. But we will have our shares or I will make him spend the best blood in his belly.'

The general confusion in the English fleet for most of the day gave the Armada breathing space. Medina Sidonia had concerns of his own, not least the degree of discipline and commitment of some of his commanders. He had been angered by the apparent flight of some of Recalde's Biscayans during the previous day's engagement, and he sent his sergeant majors and provost marshals around the fleet in pinnaces, to warn each captain in writing that 'they should put each ship in her appointed place... any ship which did not keep that order or left her appointed place that without further stay they should hang the captain of the said ship.' On balance, this seems to have been a serious overreaction, which lowered rather than buttressed Spanish morale.

In any event, no such order could save the crippled *San Salvador*. She steadily fell further and further behind the Armada, and at around 1.00 pm, Medina Sidonia ordered her to be abandoned, seemingly in a sinking condition. The remainder of her crew were taken off, together with some stores: but strangely, not the 132 barrels of powder and 2,246 rounds of shot lying in her forward hold. Late in the evening the English fleet came up with *San Salvador* and Howard, perhaps deliberately overlooking Drake, sent his cousin, Lord Thomas Howard and Sir John Hawkins to board her. They found 'a very pitiful sight, the deck of the ship fallen down, the steerage broken, the stern blown out and about fifty poor creatures burnt with powder in the most miserable sort. The stink in the ship was so unsavoury, and the sight within so ugly, that the Lord Thomas Howard and Sir John Hawkins shortly departed.'

The task of salvaging *San Salvador* was given to Captain Thomas Fleming, whose *Golden Hind* had been first to sight the Armada. He towed her into

1 August: Drake Captures the *Rosario*

Weymouth, where her powder and shot were feverishly loaded aboard a number of small vessels and carried out to the English fleet, accompanied by growing numbers of gentlemen volunteers, eager to see a piece of the action. Onshore the Cornish militia, with the threat to their county clearly at an end, were supposed to march east to reinforce other counties where the danger of a Spanish landing remained. Many, however, slipped away home to concentrate on bringing in the harvest.

Medina Sidonia meanwhile was reorganising the formation of his fleet in the light of the fighting off Plymouth. He was also concerned about the increasing possibility of being attacked frontally from the east by Lord Henry Seymour's squadron from the Straits of Dover, while Howard assaulted his rear. To guard against this the duke formed his main fighting ships into two bodies, to the front and rear of the mass of *urcas*. Pedro de Valdez's Andalusian Squadron was put under the command of Don Diego Enriquez, a son of the Viceroy of Peru, and a vanguard formed under Don Diego and the duke himself, with about twenty galleons and other fighting ships.

Don Alonso de Leiva, pending the return of Recalde, whose flagship was still sheltering among the hulks, completing repairs, was placed in charge of the rearguard, his own ships reinforced by four Portuguese galleons and all of the galleasses, giving him a total of about forty-three of the Armada's best fighting ships.

Throughout the day, at an average speed of no more than 2 or 3 knots, the rival fleets moved slowly up-Channel, watched from the cliffs and headlands by anxious throngs of people. By sunset the wind had almost completely died away, with the opposing ships drifting slowly back and forth across the expanse of Lyme Bay under the influence of the tide, just out of cannon shot range. Ahead lay Portland Bill and Weymouth and the prospect of renewed action in the morning.

The first English ship apparently to encounter the crippled *Rosario* during the night was the 300-ton armed London merchant ship *Margaret and John*. Her captain, John Nash, describes what happened:

'We only, with our ship, as all the fleet can testify, bare roomer [bore room] with the ship, being accompanied neither with ship, pinnace, or boat of all our fleet. At our approach, we found left by her, for her safeguard, a great galleon, a galleass and a pinnace, with order either to help her repair her masts, and so follow the Spanish army, gone before, or else to bring away the men, treasure and munitions thereof, and to sink or fire the ship; all which three, upon the sudden approach of our ship, only forsook Don Pedro, leaving him to the mercy of the sea. And this much hath Don Pedro himself confessed, condemning and exclaiming much upon those that were left for his comfort, that they forsook him, upon the coming of one small ship.

'About nine of the clock that same evening we came hard under the sides of the ship of Don Pedro, which by reason of her greatness, and the sea being very much grown, we could not lay aboard without spoiling our own ship. And therefore, seeing not one man show himself, nor any light appearing in her, we imagined that most of the people had been taken out; and to try whether any were aboard or not, we discharged twenty-five or thirty muskets into her cagework, at one volley, with arrows and bullet. And presently they gave us two great shot, whereupon we let fly our broadside through her, doing them some hurt, as they have and can testify.

'After this, we cast about our ship, and kept ourselves close by the Spaniard until midnight, sometimes hearing a voice in Spanish calling us, but the wind being very great, and we in the weather [upwind] the voice was carried away: that we could not well understand it, but were persuaded by our mariners to be the voice of one swimming in the sea; whereupon we put off our ship boat, with eight oars, to seek, call, and take them up, but found nobody.'

Howard's version of the capture of the *Rosario* is understandably terse:

'This night the Spanish fleet bare along by the Start [Point], and the next day, in the morning, they were as far to leeward as the Berry [Head]. Our own fleet, being disappointed of their light, by reason that Sir Francis Drake left the watch to pursue certain hulks which were descried very late in the evening, lingered behind not knowing whom to follow; only his lordship, with the *Bear* and the *Mary Rose* in his company, somewhat in his stern, pursued the enemy all night within culverin shot; his own fleet being as far behind us as, the next morning, the nearest might scarce be seen half mast high, and very many out of sight, which with a good sail recovered not his lordship the next day before it was very late in the evening. This day, Sir Francis Drake with the *Revenge*, the *Roebuck*, and a small bark or two in his company, took Don Pedro de Valdez, which was spoiled of his mast the day before; and having taken Don Pedro and certain other gentlemen, sent away the same ship and company to Dartmouth, under the conduct of the *Roebuck* and himself bare with the lord admiral, and recovered his lordship that night, being Monday.'

Medina Sidonia reported the events of the day to King Philip:

1 August: Drake Captures the *Rosario*

'Monday, 1 August, the duke ordered Don Alonso de Leiva to take the vanguard and join it to the rearguard, to form one body together with the three galleasses, and the galleons *San Mateo, San Luis, Florencia*, and *Santiago*; making that squadron now consist of the forty-three best ships of the Armada, to withstand the enemy and prevent him from standing in the way of our junction with the Duke of Parma. The Duke, with the rest of the Armada, now formed the vanguard, the whole fleet being divided into two squadrons only. The rearguard was under the command of Don Alonso de Leiva, pending the repair of Juan Martinez's [Recalde] ship, the duke in person commanding the vanguard. The duke summoned the whole of the *sargentos mayors*, and ordered each one to go in a *patache*, and take his instructions round to every ship in the Armada, specifying in writing the position they should respectively occupy. Orders were also given to them, in writing, to immediately hang any captain whose ship left its place, and they took with them the provost marshals and hangmen necessary for carrying out this order. Three *sargentos mayors* were told off for each of the two squadrons, whose duty it was to execute the aforesaid order.

'At eleven o'clock on this day the captain of Oquendo's vice-flagship came and informed the duke that the ship was foundering, and had become unmanageable. Orders were then given to tranship His Majesty's treasure, and the men on-board, the ship afterwards to be sunk.'

So ended 1 August. On balance, it had been a frustrating day for both Howard and Medina Sidonia. Thanks largely to Drake's disregard of orders, not only had Howard himself briefly been endangered, but the English fleet had been thrown into such confusion that no attack on the Armada had been possible. While it was true that two of the Armada's second line fighting ships had been captured – and more importantly, the ammunition aboard them – both were probably doomed to fall into English hands anyway.

Medina Sidonia had no obvious success to celebrate. The loss of two of his fighting ships, added to those of the earlier part of the voyage, was a serious setback. The morale of some at least of his captains was a cause for concern, and he had still had no word from Parma. At some point during the day, as hinted at in his latest message to Parma, Medina Sidonia seems to have realised the impossibility of the invasion barges meeting him off Margate. Instead, he would take the Armada close in to the French side of the Dover Straits, in the hope that Parma's flotilla could cover the relatively short distance needed to join him. In the meantime, he could only hope that, when battle was joined anew, the new organisation of his fighting ships would prove effective in beating off the English attack.

Campaign Chronicle

Tuesday 2 August: 'A Terrible Value of Great Shot' – Battle off Portland Bill

Wind and Weather: light NE to easterly wind springs up at dawn, later veering to SE then SSW; changes to southerly direction around 10.00 am; sea slight

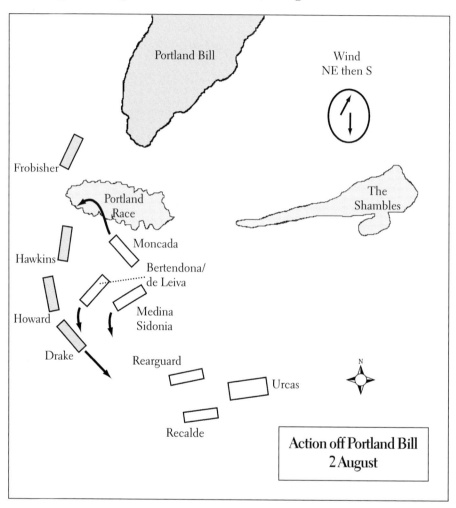

As dawn broke around 5.00 am, with Portland Bill appearing to port of both fleets through the dispersing early morning mist, a light north-easterly breeze sprang up. Though only slight, this wind direction for the first time gave the weather-gauge to the Spaniards. In an attempt to exploit the advantage, Medina Sidonia sent Miguel de Oquendo to urge Moncada to lead his galleasses, which were well suited to these conditions, in an attack on the leading English ships, offering him a Spanish estate worth 5,000 ducats a year if he did so. However,

2 August: Battle off Portland Bill

Hugo de Moncada (d.1588). An expert in galley warfare, he led the Neapolitan galleass squadron of the Armada.

whether because he was still sulking after the tiff of the previous day, or because the breeze was strengthening, Moncada declined to act.

This hesitation gave Howard time to lead a line of his galleons, close-hauled (sailing close to the wind), in a north-north-easterly direction, in an attempt to get inshore of the Spaniards, outflank their left wing and regain the advantage of the weather-gauge. However, Medina Sidonia, who had divided his van in two – part under Martin de Bertendona's command, and the remainder forming a reserve led by himself – countered by leading part of his own squadron towards Howard, barring the lord admiral's inshore passage about 4 miles from Portland Bill, and forcing the English commander to come about on the opposite tack, and head south-east in an attempt to engage the starboard wing of the Armada, with a view to outflanking it on the seaward side.

This move offered an opportunity for the Spanish rearguard to attack him, and two battlegroups – led by de Leiva in his *Rata*, and Martin de Bertendona in *Regazona* – aided by other vessels, including galleons and ships of the Levant Squadron, cut across Howard's path opened fire. With the advantage of the

Campaign Chronicle

Miguel de Oquendo (d.1588). Commander of the Squadron of Guipuzcoa and a courageous fighter.

weather-gauge, the Spaniards were able to close within musket range, and it seemed at one point as if *Regazona* was about to board one large English vessel, perhaps *Ark Royal* herself. However, with the usual English superior nimbleness and speed, the intended target pulled clear.

By 9.00 am, a full-scale action was in progress, with the English ships standing their ground and exchanging shots until the Spaniards came too near, when they drew off, led by *Ark Royal*, and also including the *Elizabeth Jonas* and the *Nonpareil*: the English ships presenting their sterns to the enemy in what, in a later age, would be known as a simultaneous turn-away. Planned tactics are difficult to discern. Both sides seem to have exchanged one or more broadsides at close range and then continued more sporadic fire at a longer range for upwards of an hour, with Howard's ships constantly evading Spanish attempts to board, but at the same time reducing the effects of their own gunnery by engaging at too long a range.

However, while this action was still continuing, the Spaniards noticed that a squadron of half a dozen English ships had apparently continued to work close in to the shore in an attempt to outflank the Spaniards, but seemingly having

Ordnance

I n general terms, both fleets employed the same types of ordnance. On balance, many of the English guns were of better quality, which together with superior handling techniques, gave their gunners a distinct advantage.

There is often some confusion about the exact ranges of the different guns. Measurement of this was often expressed in terms of 'paces', but there was some variation in exactly what this represented. The most likely definition is the equivalent of about 1 yard (slightly less than 1 metre).

The guns employed in the campaign can be divided into two broad categories: heavy muzzle-loading ship smashers, and small, breech-loading anti-personnel weapons.

Gun	Calibre (inches)	Weight of Shot (pounds)	Range: point-blank/extreme (paces)	English totals	Spanish totals
Cannon	7.25	50	340/2,000	} 55	66
Demi-cannon	6.25	32	340/1,700		
Cannon-perier	8	24	320/1,600	43	326
Culverin	5.25	17	400/2.400	153	165
Demi-culverin	4.25	9	400/2,500	344	137
Saker	3.25	5	340/1,700	662	144
Minion	3.25	4	320/1,600	715	189
Total guns over 4 lb				1,972	1,124
Number of gun-carrying ships				172	124
Average weight of shot per ship				85 lb	156 lb
Total weight of shot thrown				14,677 lb	19,369 lb

misjudged the distance, now appeared to be hemmed in and trapped by the out-jutting Portland Bill. The squadron was headed by Martin Frobisher in his *Triumph*, the largest ship in the English fleet, whose high superstructures made her seem even bigger than was in fact the case. With her were the armed London merchant ships *Merchant Royal*, John Nash's *Margaret and John*, the *Centurion* and the *Golden Lion*, together with the *Mary Rose*.

Opinion remains divided as to whether Frobisher was attempting a finely judged manoeuvre designed to lure the enemy into a trap or if he had in fact made an error and placed himself in difficulties. However, apparently running out of sea room, and unable to pull clear unless the wind direction changed, he had been forced to drop anchor in the same difficult situation that Howard had avoided by going about. The fact remains that Frobisher probably knew the waters of the English Channel better than many of the other English commanders. If there was any advantage to be gained from tide or current, he could be expected to be aware of it, and to act accordingly.

To Medina Sidonia, the situation offered a seemingly heaven-sent opportunity to destroy part of the infuriatingly elusive English fleet. The Spanish van, with de Leiva and Bertendona, were for now too far to the north-east to engage Frobisher, but with the breeze perhaps dropping slightly, it was an excellent opportunity for the galleasses, moving under sail and perhaps also oars. The duke addressed Moncada in person, in an apparently frosty exchange, during which Medina Sidonia evidently suggested that a second failure to carry out orders would reflect seriously upon Moncada's honour. The galleass commander, perhaps reluctantly, agreed to engage Frobisher.

Presenting a colourful and dashing spectacle with their red and gold painted superstructures and their blood-red oars flashing as they beat the water, the galleasses, supported by three or four more fighting ships nearby, advanced to battle. However, as Moncada came within range, he seemed to falter. To an angry Medina Sidonia, it seemed that once again his galleass commander was failing to press home an attack. He fumed later: 'A fine day this had been. If the galleasses had come up as I expected, the enemy would have had his fill.' In fact he was accusing Moncada unfairly.

As Frobisher certainly knew – and probably counted on – the waters around Portland Bill had strong eddies and currents, particularly at ebb and flood tides. Just to the east of the Bill, the Shambles, an area of sandbanks and shallows, formed a serious hazard to unwary shipping, while the feared Portland Race, a tidal 'rip', ran between the Shambles and the Bill. The current here could reach a speed of 7 knots at full tide, while beneath an apparently placid surface, constantly shifting currents created fierce turbulence.

Once they entered the fringes of the Race the galleasses were in trouble. Unable to make progress under sail, and with their oar banks disrupted both by the currents and by enemy fire, their advance faltered. Frobisher, meanwhile, presenting the Spaniards with his broadsides, was apparently motionless in the seemingly still water where the tidal eddy ran. Moncada's vessels could only engage the English after crossing the fierce waters of the Race. They tried several times, but failed, the rough water threatening to swamp them and sweeping them back. An eyewitness aboard the galleass *Zúñiga* was involved in the engagement with Frobisher:

2 August: Battle off Portland Bill

'While we were attacking the great ship of the enemy [the *Triumph*] and two other ships, five of the enemy's galleons bore down upon our galleasses, the wind at this time having suddenly shifted, so that the enemy had it astern whilst we had it against us, and consequently none of our ships could come to our aid. The galleasses therefore had to run and join the rest of the Armada.'

At the same time, the galleasses were coming under heavy fire from Frobisher's ships, which were probably turning using their figure of eight tactics, in order to bring all their guns to bear. Nevertheless, neither side appears to have suffered serious damage, and at about 1.00 pm the wind changed, and a light southerly breeze sprang up.

This wind change was common at that time of day, and at once altered the tactical situation. The main area of fighting had hitherto been slipping slowly back in a westerly direction towards Lyme Bay, with neither fleet gaining a decided advantage. But the change in wind direction once again gave the weather-gauge to the English ships, and their commanders, who had probably been anticipating the wind change, were quick to respond. Howard reversed course, taking his main body back in a northerly direction in order to support Frobisher.

The van of the Armada, under Medina Sidonia and Bertendona, seem at this point to have been heading south, still exchanging fire with Howard. The wind change probably forced them to turn slightly to the south-east. Now Drake's squadron, which had hitherto played little part in the action, took advantage of the change in wind direction to attack the seaward side of the Armada, where the rear, probably again under Recalde's command, was stationed. Recalde's *San Juan* was soon hotly engaged with Drake's leading ships, as 'a troop of Her Majesty's ships and sundry merchants assaulted the Spanish fleet so sharply to the westward that they were all forced to give way and bear room.' Pedro Estrade, aboard *San Mateo*, could see much of the action: 'We gave chase to the enemy, the galleasses with some other ships wearing into them, playing with their ordnance, turning in the wind from the south-west to the south-east, fighting with us, and there was good store of cannon shot. The flagship of Juan Martinez de Recalde came entering in from the south-east, and with him Juan Gomez de Medina in the *Gran Grifon*, flagship of the hulks, and other ships, we came so nigh unto the enemy vice admiral that with one piece of cast iron we shot two bullets into the vice admiral of the English, and there was great shot of ordnance.'

Seeing his rear crumpling under the attack of some fifty English ships, Medina Sidonia for the first time that day had cause for alarm – the early fighting having, perhaps, tipped slightly in favour of the Spanish. Howard had taken advantage of the confusion caused by Drake's attack to renew his attempt to break through to Frobisher, but the duke, with his flagship, the Portuguese galleons, and five other vessels, moved to block his path. But then, seeing the growing confusion on the Spanish right, Medina Sidonia detached his force – apart from his flagship – to support Recalde, and took the *San Martin* alone to engage Howard.

Both fleets were probably by now in a state of some confusion. Most of de Leiva's and Bertendona's battlegroups were involved in supporting Recalde on the eastern side of the battle, leaving Medina Sidonia in the *San Martin* in an exposed situation. Howard was unable to bring all his squadron into action, but the *San Martin* was still faced by *Ark Royal* herself, supported by *Elizabeth Jonas, Galleon Leicester, Golden Lion, Victory, Mary Rose, Dreadnought* and *Swallow*.

In a typically unrealistic gesture of chivalry, Medina Sidonia lowered his topsails, inviting the English to engage. They needed no encouragement, and closed to within 'half musket range' – probably around 100 yards. A furious engagement began, with the English ships approaching in turn to fire off their bow chasers, their broadsides, and their stern guns as they drew off. Medina Sidonia reckoned later that 500 shots had been aimed at *San Martin*, while she managed to fire about eighty in response, during an engagement of around an hour and a half. Nevertheless, the English were evidently still not engaging at close enough range to inflict really telling damage. The *San Martin* suffered some injury to her rigging, sails, and masts, and the Holy Banner she flew was ripped in two by a shot: but there were no reports of serious injury to her hull. But an anonymous English participant found the engagement a terrifying experience:

'There never was seen so vehement a fight, either side endeavouring, through a headstrong and deadly hatred, the other's spoil and destruction. Although the musketeers and arquebusiers were in either fleet in number, yet could they not be discerned or heard, by reason of the more violent and roaring shot of the greater ordnance, that followed so thick one upon the other… Blaze of burning darts flying to and fro, leams of stars coruscant, streams and hails of fiery sparks, lightenings of wildfire on water and land. Flight and shoot of thunderbolts all with such countenance, terror and vehemence, that the heavens thundered, the waters surged, the earth shook.'

Calderon watched the duel between San Martin and Howard's squadron:

'She was reinforced by Oquendo's flagship [the *Santa Ana*] which managed to join her and help her gallantly in her brave fight. The *San Martin* fired over eighty shots from one side only, and inflicted great damage on the enemy. The latter shot at the duke at least 500 cannon balls, some of which struck his hull and others his rigging, carrying away his flagstaff and one of the stays of his mainmast.'

Eventually, at around 2.30 pm, de Leiva's battlegroup was able to come to Medina Sidonia's support, and covered by the galleon *San Marcos* and the *Santa Ana*, the flagship pulled back into the main body of the Armada.

Fighting was now dying down. Bertendona's battlegroup had probably come to the assistance of Recalde, and Drake's attack, which never seems to have been pressed very closely, petered out in indecisive long-range fire, which continued for most of the afternoon. The freshening breeze, meanwhile, had allowed Frobisher to pull clear of Portland Bill and rejoin Howard, and with the end of serious fighting, it was again time for the opposing commanders to consider its results. Medina Sidonia related the day's events to King Philip:

'Tuesday 2 August, broke fine, the enemy's fleet being to leeward, sailing towards the land, and making great efforts to gain the wind of us. The duke also tacked towards the land and tried to keep the wind. He led, followed by the galleasses, the rest of the Armada being somewhat more distant, and the enemy, noticing the duke's flagship was approaching the land and that it was impossible to get to windward of her that way, put about to seaward and sailed on the opposite tack. Our ships, being to windward of the enemy, then attacked him. The enemy's flagship then turned tail and put her head seaward, and the following of our ships also attacked him and endeavoured to close with him, namely: the *San Marcos, San Luis, San Mateo, La Rata*, Oquendo [presumably Oquendo's flagship, *Santa Ana*], *San Felipe, San Juan de Sicilia*, with Don Diego Tellez Enriquez on-board (which ship had been near the enemy since morning), the galleon *Florencia*, the galleon *Santiago*, the galleon *San Juan*, with Don Diego Enriquez, son of the Viceroy of Portugal, on-board, and the Levant ship *Valencera*, with the maestre de campo, Don Alonso de Luzon, on-board. The vanguard galleasses approached quite close to the enemy, thanks to the current, and the duke sent them orders to make every effort to close – using both sail and oar.

'The duke's flagship also turned to attack. The galleasses caught up with some ships of the enemy, having got quite close to the enemy for the purpose of boarding. But it was all useless, for when the enemy saw that our intention was to come to close quarters with him, he sheered off to seaward, his great advantage being in the swiftness of his ships. Soon afterwards, the enemy's ships returned with the wind and tide in their favour, and attacked Juan Martinez de Recalde in the rearguard. Don Alonso de Leiva reinforced the latter, and our flagship, which was then in the midst of the main squadron, sailed to the support of the ships of the Armada, which were mixed up with the enemy's rearguard and separated from the mass of both fleets. The duke ordered Captain Marolin to go in a *felucca* and try to guide the vessels, which were near the duke's flagship, to the support of Juan Martinez de Recalde. When this was effected the enemy left Juan Martinez, and attacked the duke's flagship, which was isolated and on her way to the assistance of the said ships.

'When our flagship saw that the flagship of the enemy was leading towards her, she lowered her topsails, and the enemy's flagship passed her, followed by the whole of his fleet, each ship firing at our flagship as it passed. The guns on our flagship were served well and rapidly, and by the time half of the enemy's fleet had passed her the firing became more distant. The flagship was reinforced by Juan Martinez de Recalde, Don Alonso de Leiva, the Marquis de Penatal, in the *San Marcos*, and Oquendo, although by the time they came up the hottest fury was past. The enemy then put about to seaward. We watched the enemy's flagship retreating and she appeared to have suffered some damage. The enemy's vessels that were engaged with our vanguard were also withdrawn. One of the most forward of our ships in this three hours' skirmish was the galleon *Florencia*.'

Lord Howard described the action from the English viewpoint:

'The next morning, being Tuesday, 23 July 1588 [3 August NS], the wind sprang up at north-east, and then the Spaniards had the wind of the English army [fleet], which stood in the north-westward, towards the shore. So did the Spaniards also. But that course was not good for the English army to recover the wind of the Spaniards, and therefore they cast about to the eastwards; whereupon the Spaniards bare room, offering [to] board our ships. Upon which coming room there grew a great fight. The English ships stood fast and abode their coming, and the enemy, seeing us to abide them, and divers of our ships to stay for them, as the *Ark*, the *Nonpareil*, the *Elizabeth Jonas*, the *Victory*, etc., and divers other ships, they were content to fall astern of the *Nonpareil*, which was the sternmost ship. In the meantime, the *Triumph*, with five ships, viz., the *Merchant Royal*, the *Centurion*, the *Margaret and John*, the *Mary Rose*, and the *Golden Lion*, were so far to leeward and separated from our fleet, that the galleasses took courage and bare room with them and assaulted them sharply. But they were very well resisted by those ships for the space of an hour and a half. At length, certain of Her Majesty's ships bare with them, and then the galleasses forsook them.

'The wind then shifted to the south-eastwards and so to SSW, at what time a troop of Her Majesty's ships and sundry merchants' assailed the Spanish fleet so sharply from the westward that they were all forced to give way and to bare room; which his lordship perceived, together with the distress that the *Triumph* and the five merchant ships in her company were in, called unto certain of Her Majesty's ships then near at hand and charged them straitly to follow him, and to set freshly upon the Spaniards, and to go within musket shot of the enemy before they should discharge any one piece of ordnance, thereby to succour the *Triumph*; which was very well performed by the *Ark*, the *Elizabeth Jonas*, the *Galleon of Leicester*, the *Golden Lion*, the *Victory*, the *Mary Rose*, the *Dreadnought* and the *Swallow*: for so they went in order into the fight. Which the Duke of Medina perceiving, came out with sixteen of his best galleons, to impeach his lordship and to stop him from assisting of the *Triumph*. At which assault, after wonderful sharp conflict, the Spaniards were forced to give way and to flock together like sheep. In this conflict one William Coxe, captain of a small pinnace of Sir William Wynter's, named the *Delight*, showed himself most valiant in the face of his enemies at the hottest of the encounter, where afterwards lost his life in the service with a great shot.

'Towards the evening, some four or five ships of the Spanish fleet edged out of the south-westwards, where some other of our ships met them, amongst which *Mayflower of London* discharged some pieces at them very valiantly, which ship and company at sundry other times behaved themselves eminently.

'This fight was very nobly continued from morning until evening, the lord admiral being always in the hottest of the encounter, and it may well be said that for the time there was never seen a more terrible value of great shot, nor more hot fight than this was; for although the musketeers and arquebusiers of crock [firing with musket rests] were then infinite, yet could they not be discerned nor heard for that the great ordnance came so thick that a man would have judged it to have been a hot skirmish of small shot, being all the fight long within half musket shot of the enemy.'

The councils of war called by the opposing commanders that evening had unpalatable realities to digest. Medina Sidonia was annoyed and frustrated. Though he and most of his commanders had fought skilfully and hard, he was, probably unjustly, dissatisfied with the performance of Moncada and the galleasses, from which so much had been hoped at the start of the campaign.

Campaign Chronicle

The hard fighting of the day had once again demonstrated the inability of the Spanish ships to close near enough to the enemy to board them. The duke commented in a letter to Parma that 'some of our ships have been in the very midst of the enemy's fleet, to entice one of his ships to grapple and begin the fight, but all to no purpose.' In exasperation, he remarked to his officers: 'These people do not mean to fight, but only to delay our progress.'

It seems as if that morning, with the rare advantage of the weather-gauge, Medina Sidonia had lost sight of his instructions from the king to avoid battle unless faced with no alternative, and had been unable to resist the lure of Frobisher and his squadron. But the only result had been to fire off a great deal of valuable ammunition, and delay his progress towards an uncertain rendezvous with Parma, from whom he still had heard nothing.

Howard also had serious food for thought. Whether or not Frobisher had been baiting a trap, or more likely got himself into a tight spot, English operations throughout the day had showed a notable lack of coordination, with senior commanders like Drake and Frobisher – and even individual captains – acting on their own initiative. As a result, there had been little attempt to concentrate the main strength of the English fleet in decisive attacks on the enemy, whose formation had once again remained largely unbroken.

Howard knew that within a couple of days the Armada would be approaching the Isle of Wight, the last place in which the Spanish fleet could find anchorage before it reached the Straits of Dover. His fleet was constantly being joined by a trickle of small vessels from each little port it passed, and though some brought welcome supplies of ammunition, these reinforcements were, on the whole, of little fighting value, and merely added to the general inability to coordinate attacks.

Just out of gunshot range of each other, the opposing fleets drifted eastwards on a gentle breeze through the night, most on-board aware that the decisive stage of the campaign was approaching.

Wednesday 3 August: Frustration for Howard
Wind and Weather: wind SSW, light; sea calm
At first light, with the Armada off the Dorset coast, renewed action seemed likely. During the night, the 650-ton *Gran Grin*, vice admiral of the Biscayan Squadron, had dropped behind the rest of the Spanish fleet. As dawn broke, her captain, Juan Gomez de Medina, saw Drake's *Revenge* bearing down on him. Following the customary English tactics, Drake fired one broadside into the Spanish vessel, went about and fired the other, then pulled under *Gran Grin*'s stern and raked her with musket fire. Other English ships came up to join in the battle, while some of the Spanish battlegroups of Recalde, de Leiva, and

76

3 August: Frustration for Howard

Bertendona turned back in support of the stricken *Gran Grin*. The Spanish ship was apparently no longer answering to her rudder, but as the conflict widened, a galleass managed to get a tow line to de Medina's vessel and pull her to safety. The other galleasses engaged *Revenge,* and claimed to have brought down her main yard and damaged her rigging.

Spain's 'Venganza'

F oremost in the battle against the Armada – and remarked on by friend and foe – had been the queen's 'race-built' galleon *Revenge*, seen by the Spaniards as being 'one of the finest galleons in the world'. Ironically, she was the only one of the queen's major vessels to be lost due to enemy action in the entire war, and provided the Spaniards with one of their few victories at sea.

In May 1591, a squadron under Thomas, Lord Howard, was despatched to the Azores in a bid to capture the *flota* returning from the New World. Among Howard's vessels was *Revenge*, commanded by Sir Richard Grenville. Arrogant, brutally ruthless, and so fiercely ambitious that his attitude at times verged on insanity, Grenville had been ashore during the Armada campaign, and was thirsty for glory.

Howard's expedition suffered an early blow when it was discovered that some of the Spanish treasure ships had evaded them. However, the English commanders wrongly believed that the main *flota* was still approaching the Azores, and resolved to lie in wait.

Unbeknown to the English, the Spanish authorities were making feverish preparations to meet and escort home the remainder of the *flota*. In Ferrol, The captain-general of the fleet, Alonso de Bazan (brother to the late Marquis of Santa Cruz), was hastily fitting out a powerful force of thirty warships, including six of the new 'Apostles': 'race-built' galleons of the English pattern. Among his squadron commanders was Armada veteran, Martin de Bertendona.

Thirsting for vengeance, the Spanish commanders saw an opportunity to surprise the unwary English squadron in the Azores, and during the night of 29–30 August, Bazan, dividing his fleet into two squadrons, closed in on the English anchorage off the island of Flores. The Spaniards were delayed by light winds, and at about 5.00 pm, as they approached the English squadron, a horrified Howard realised the danger he faced.

The English squadron hastily raised sail, and all – except *Revenge* – narrowly evaded the trap. It remains unclear whether Grenville, *contd over*

Spain's 'Venganza' *continued*

waiting to pick up a shore party, was simply too late to escape, or whether he chose to make a daring dash across the bows of the leading Spanish vessels in an act of insane bravado. The outcome was the same. Cut off from safety, *Revenge* faced the fury of the entire Spanish fleet.

The Spaniards had watched with amazement, as Grenville, 'valuing the world as nothing [advanced] towards our fleet with *arogancia'*. In another display of half-crazed chivalry, Grenville chose not to attempt to make proper use of his heavy guns to fight a stand-off engagement, but gave the Spaniards their dearest wish, by closing for their long-desired action at close quarters.

During the next twelve hours one of the epic 'last stands' of maritime history was fought out. Closing with the 'Apostle', *San Felipe*, Grenville – with no more than about 200 men fit for action – savagely mauled the first waves of borders, and battered the Spaniard with his cannon. Then Bertendona's 'Apostle', *San Barnabe*, joined in the fight, lashing herself to *Revenge*, and sweeping her decks with musketry.

Far into the night the fight went on. Grenville, though wounded (likened by the Spaniards to 'the brave bull that was so full of blood and courage'), led his psalm-singing crewmen in hurling back repeated boarding attacks. More Spanish vessels joined in the battle, lashing themselves to the stricken *Revenge*.

As his men fell around him, the seriously wounded Grenville continued to call out: 'Fight on! Fight on! No surrender!' Several hundred Spaniards fell in their unsuccessful assaults, while more men perished on two ships that went down as a result of damage.

However, as dawn broke, *Revenge* herself lay a dismasted water-logged wreck, surrounded by the enemy. Grenville, dying from his wounds, threatened to blow up his ship rather than surrender, but was deserted by most of his surviving men, who fled in boats to take refuge with the enemy.

Revenge was renamed *La Venganza* by her triumphant captors, who had paid such a high price for their victory. They would not enjoy her possession for long. On 15 September, returning to Spain, the fleet was hit by a violent storm – seen by some as Grenville's retribution from beyond the grave – during which *Revenge* along with a dozen Spanish vessels, was dashed to pieces on the rocks of the island of Terciera.

3 August: Frustration for Howard

Medina Sidonia arrived at the scene of the action, and once again dipped his topsails in an invitation to battle. Howard, however, responded by pulling the English fleet back out of range. Most probably he was motivated by concern over his stocks of ammunition, and the result was that the fight, not thought worth mentioning by Howard in his account, died down. It had, however, been sharp while it lasted, costing *Gran Grin* sixty dead and seventy wounded. The Spanish ship had been hit by at least forty cannon shot, while musket balls found embedded in her hull testified to the close range at which much of the action had been fought.

In the afternoon, the breeze, which had been light all morning, died away, and as the fleets drifted slowly off The Needles, at the western end of the Isle of Wight, Howard called a council of war. The indecisive nature of the day's fighting, and the knowledge that next day was likely to witness a major action for possession of the Isle of Wight, had evidently convinced Howard that the English fleet needed to be reorganised. He divided it into four squadrons, each consisting of approximately twenty-five ships, commanded by himself, Drake, Frobisher, and Hawkins.

Howard's intention was to test the new organisation by launching an attack on the Armada's rear during the night, using some armed merchant ships – probably with the hope of disrupting the Spanish fleet sufficiently to frustrate any attempt next day to make a landing on the Isle of Wight. But the design was frustrated by lack of wind, as the rival fleets drifted slowly on eastwards. At least Howard's concerns about ammunition were slightly eased during the day, as a stream of small craft joined him carrying supplies, many of them taken from the two captured Spanish ships.

Medina Sidonia's version of events was as follows:

'Wednesday, the 3rd, Juan Martinez de Recalde again assumed command of the rearguard, Don Alonso de Leiva remaining with him, the forty odd ships that formed the rearguard being divided between them. At dawn the enemy were near our rear, the vice-flagship receiving some cannon fire from him. Our galleasses fired their stern guns, Juan Martinez', Don Alonso de Leiva's, and the rest of the rear squadron did likewise without leaving their positions, and the enemy then retired without attempting anything further; our galleasses having disabled the rigging of the enemy's flagship, and brought down his mainsail boom.'

Howard had even less to report:

'The next day, being Wednesday 24 July [3 August NS] 1588, there was little done, for that in the fight on Sunday and Tuesday much of our munition had been spent, and therefore the lord admiral sent divers barks and pinnaces unto the shore for a new supply of such provisions. This day the lord admiral divided his fleet into four squadrons, whereof he appointed the first to attend himself; the second his lordship committed to the charge of Sir Francis Drake; the third to Sir John Hawkins, and the fourth to Sir Martin Frobisher. This afternoon his lordship gave order that, in the night, six merchant ships out of every squadron should set upon the Spanish fleet in sundry places, at one instant, in the night time, to keep the enemy waking; but all that night fell out to be so calm that nothing could be done.'

Nothing had happened during the day greatly to change the overall situation. The Armada had continued on course, with no news from Parma, but neither had the English been able to inflict any more damage on the Spanish ships. So far, the Spanish plan appeared to be succeeding. Howard had little cause for satisfaction. He had expended huge amounts of ammunition during the two principal engagements fought so far, without being able to divert the Spaniards from their course. Time was running out if they were to be stopped before joining Parma, and in the immediate future, there was the growing fear that the Armada might seize a base in the Solent. What happened next day would be critical.

Thursday 4 August: Battle for the Solent

Wind and Weather: light winds, probably from the west; sea calm

For the past four centuries debate has raged regarding Medina Sidonia's intentions on this day. Did he plan to copy the example of the French, four decades earlier, and occupy the Isle of Wight – or at least secure the great anchorage of the Solent? Or had he decided to follow his instructions from King Philip, and continue without diversion to link up with Parma in the Straits of Dover? There are arguments in favour of both possibilities. The duke was still anxiously awaiting news from Parma, but the failure of any messages to arrive may have tilted him towards the Isle of Wight option. If this was indeed the case, involving as it did, direct disobedience to Philip's orders, it is hardly surprising the duke made no mention of such intentions in his reports to the king or letters to Parma. On balance, it seems likely that Medina Sidonia was keeping all his options open that morning.

The English, however, anticipated that the Spaniards would make an attempt on the Isle of Wight. Elizabeth's privy council had already concluded that the island was a tempting objective for the enemy: 'First, where he may find the least

4 August: Battle for the Solent

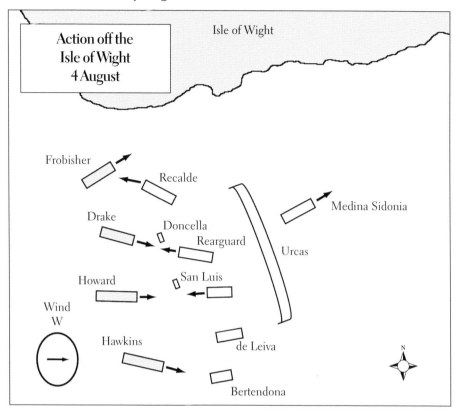

Action off the
Isle of Wight
4 August

Isle of Wight

Frobisher

Recalde

Medina Sidonia

Drake

Doncella

Rearguard

Urcas

Howard

San Luis

Wind
W

Hawkins

de Leiva

N

Bertendona

resistance, and most quiet landing. Secondly, where he may have best harbour for his galleys and speediest supplies out of Spain, France and Flanders. Thirdly, where he may most offend the realm by incursions…'

Some 9,000 militia were massed to defend the anchorage of Southampton, while 3,000 more, commanded by the governor, Sir George Carey, were on the alert throughout the night on the Isle of Wight, their ears straining in the darkness for the splashing sound of Spanish oars, signifying the arrival of enemy landing parties. Few, least of all Carey, had any illusions of the likely outcome if veteran Spanish troops secured a bridgehead.

As dawn approached, Howard and his commanders knew that the next few hours would be critical. If Medina Sidonia were to attempt to enter St Helens Roads, at the approaches to the Solent at the eastern end of the Isle of Wight, the tide would only be in his favour between 7.00 am to about noon. After that the current would be flowing too strongly against him to make entry possible.

As the early morning light strengthened, the first sights to greet the anxious English were the Portuguese galleon, *San Luis de Portugal*, and the *Duquesne Santa Ana* of the Andalusian Squadron, which appeared to be straggling behind the

Top left: A caliver man. Top right: A musketeer. Note that the musket, unlike the caliver, has to be fired with the aid of a 'rest', because of its length and weight.
Below: A pikeman. Those operating aboard ships normally employed a half-pike or a pole-type weapon such as a halberd.

4 August: Battle for the Solent

Sir John Hawkins (1532–95). A 'rough, masterful man', he was at various times a merchant, slave trader, and privateer.

main body of the Armada. Once again, there has been considerable discussion as to whether these two vessels were genuine stragglers who had become detached during the night, or whether they were being employed as bait by Medina Sidonia: either in an attempt to draw some English ships into a trap, or to bring on an action in which the Spanish rear would hold off the English fleet long enough for the duke and the van squadron to enter the Solent. It may be that the continuing near-calm had caused Medina Sidonia to see an opportunity for his galleasses to repeat the mauling that he felt they had inflicted on the previous day.

Hawkins led the English squadron nearest the stragglers, and with insufficient wind to propel his ships, manned his longboats in order to tow his flagship, *Victory*, within range. As the English came within musket shot, three of the galleasses – supporting the idea that Medina Sidonia had laid a trap – came rowing into view, towing with them *La Rata Encoronada* for extra firepower. On the English side, Lord Thomas Howard's galleon, *Golden Lion*, was also being towed into action, and his example was followed by the lord admiral himself in *Ark Royal*.

A superficially fierce-looking engagement followed, though little real damage was inflicted by either side. The English claimed that, of the galleasses, 'one of them was fain to be carried away on the careen [possibly holed and listing, or merely having shifted men and contents in order to increase the angle of fire of her guns on that side].' Another lost her stern lantern 'which came swimming by' and another lost 'her nose' – presumably her ram. The Spanish officer aboard the galleass, *Zúñiga*, writes of the opening stages of the action: 'The English would certainly have captured the hulk *Santa Ana* if the three galleasses *San Lorenzo*, *Zúñiga* and *Girona* had not at once gone to her rescue. In order to save her, they had to engage over thirty of the enemy's ships.'

None of this was sufficient to put any of the galleasses permanently out of action, and now, as a light breeze, sprang up, more ships became involved in the fighting. As at Portland, Frobisher's squadron occupied a position close inshore, its commander, with his detailed knowledge of the currents of these coastal waters, evidently being given the task of trying to slip past the inshore flank of the Armada, get ahead, and bar the entrance to the Solent. Even before the breeze freshened, the current was carrying him along at the rate of about 1 knot, more rapidly than the Spanish vessels further out to sea.

At this point, probably around 9.00 am, Howard was off Dunnose Point, and to leeward of the Spanish van. He was evidently engaged with Medina Sidonia's *San Martin*, which, as usual, had been among the first reinforcements to join the galleasses: 'At the same time that this conflict was in our rear, the enemy admiral and other great ships assailed our *capitana*. They came closer than on the previous day, firing off their heaviest guns from the lowest deck, cutting the trice of our mainmast and killing some of our soldiers.' This suggests that the English fleet was now engaging the enemy at significantly closer range than previously, and perhaps making more use of their heavier lower-deck guns than in the earlier actions. There was good reason for this effort, as the next few hours would decide whether the Spaniards could enter the Solent.

Frobisher's role during this critical period would be vital, but in the earlier part of the morning, with no wind, he seemed once again to be in serious danger. For a time he was engaged with the *San Martin* and the galleass *San Lorenzo*, and seemed likely to be trapped. All available boats – about eleven in all – from the other ships in Frobisher's squadron (themselves evidently not closely threatened), were sent to tow *Triumph* to safety.

It has been suggested that Frobisher was attempting to draw the Spaniards into St Catherine's Race, an area of treacherous currents and shallows, where the

4 August: Battle for the Solent

Action off the Isle of Wight. The Rata Encoronada *was actually towed by a galleass, not by ships' boats.*

tide ran at 6 or 7 knots, but the evidence is inconclusive. He may just as easily have misjudged speed and distance and put himself in serious peril. The Spaniards believed this to be the case. Medina Sidonia was 'certain that we would this day succeed in boarding them, wherein was the only way to victory.' Indeed, he asserted, *Triumph* 'had been so spoiled in the fight, that she struck her standard and discharged pieces to show her need of succour.'

However, in the nick of time a breeze sprang up, shifting around to the south-west, and enabling Lord Sheffield's *White Bear*, with the *Elizabeth Jonas*, to come to Frobisher's assistance. With the wind now in her favour, *Triumph* hoisted every available sail, and headed for the safety of the rest of Frobisher's squadron. Several Spanish ships attempted to intercept her, but, as Calderon admitted: 'the galleon *San Juan de Portugal* and another quick-sailing ship – the speediest vessels in the Armada – although they gave chase, seemed in comparison with her to be standing still.'

Meanwhile, with the freshening south-westerly breeze restoring the weather-gauge to the English fleet, Howard and Drake's squadrons engaged the seaward wing of the Armada, attacking some of the ships of Medina Sidonia's rear squadron. The first impact of their assault fell on the 34-gun Portuguese galleon *San Mateo*, and the 961-ton *Florencia*, with fifty-two pieces the heaviest-gunned ship of the Armada. More ships on both sides soon became engaged, and 'After wonderful sharp conflict the Spaniards were forced to give way and to flock together like sheep.'

It is sometimes proposed the English plan was to drive the Spaniards on to the Owers Bank, a series of rocky shallows that extended out to sea just to the east of the entrance to the Solent. However, suggestions the Spaniards were ignorant of this hazard – which was well-known to all who used the Channel – seem doubtful. In any case, while the Armada was still perhaps half an hour away from the dangers of the Owers Bank, Medina Sidonia ordered the fleet to bear on a south-south-easterly course, further out into the Channel, and the action came to an end.

Sir George Cary, governor of the Isle of Wight, watched the conclusion of the engagement with relief: 'The fleets kept the direct trade and shot into the sea out of our sight by three of the clock this afternoon; whereupon we have dissolved our camp wherein we have continued since Monday.'

The English were anxious to conserve their limited supplies of ammunition, and the Spaniards had, in any case, now been carried too far to the east of the Solent to make any attempt at entering it feasible.

As the Isle of Wight receded behind him that afternoon, Medina Sidonia's main concern remained the lack of any news from Parma. Once again the duke wrote urgently to the commander of the Army of Flanders, reporting another frustrating action in which the Spaniards had seemed near to gaining a significant success, only for the English to retire beyond boarding distance: 'Sometimes some of our ships have been in the very midst of the enemy's fleet, to induce one of his ships to grapple and begin the fight, but all to no purpose, because his ships are very light and mine very heavy.' To add to the duke's worries: 'The enemy has plenty of men and stores. My stores are beginning to run short with these constant skirmishes, and if the weather does not improve and the enemy

4 August: Battle for the Solent

Battle off the Isle of Wight. Dunnose was the sixteenth-century name for St Catherine's Point on the Isle of Wight.

continues his tactics, as he certainly will, it will be advisable for Your Excellency to load a couple of ships with powder and ball of the size and total in the enclosed memorandum and despatch them to me without delay. It will also be advisable for Your Excellency to make ready at once to put out to meet us, because, by God's grace, if the wind serves, I intend to be on the Flemish coast very soon.'

Medina Sidonia's note specified a need for shot of 4, 5 and 10 pounds in weight. Equally significant was his intention – now made clear – to abandon the idea of a rendezvous with Parma off the 'Cape of Margate' and instead join with him much nearer to the coast of Flanders. This may have signified partial recognition of the formidable nature of the English fleet, and the impossibility of Parma's invasion flotilla making an unsupported attempt to cross the Channel. The duke, however, clearly assumed that Parma's invasion flotilla would be able to brush past any blockading Dutch or English, and join him in the open sea. The misunderstanding that King Philip had feared would wreck the entire enterprise was ominously apparent.

Medina Sidonia's description of the action is worth quoting at length:

Campaign Chronicle

'Thursday, the 4th, St Dominic's day, the hulk *Santa Ana* and a galleon of Portugal had fallen somewhat astern, and were fiercely attacked by the enemy. The galleasses – Don Alonso de Leiva's, and other ships – came to their assistance. Although the two ships were surrounded by many enemies, the galleasses were successful in bringing them out. Whilst the skirmish was going on in the rear, the enemy's flagship, with other large vessels, fell upon our royal flagship, which was leading the vanguard. They came closer than on the previous day, firing off their heaviest guns from the lowest deck, cutting the trice of our mainmast, and killing some of our soldiers. The *San Luis*, with the maestre de campo Don Agustin [Mexia] on-board, came to the rescue, and the enemy was also faced by Juan Martinez de Recalde, the *San Juan* of Diego Flores' squadron, with Don Diego Enriquez on-board, and Oquendo, who placed himself before our flagship, as the current made it impossible for him to stand alongside. Other vessels did likewise, although the enemy retired.

'The enemy's flagship [the *Triumph*] had suffered considerable damage, and had drifted somewhat to leeward of our armada. Our flagship then turned upon her, supported by Juan Martinez de Recalde, the *San Juan de Sicilia*, the flagship of the galleons of Castile, the *Gran Grin* and the rest of our ships. To windward of us was the enemy's fleet coming up to support their flagship, which was in such straits that she had to be towed out by eleven long boats, lowering her standard and firing guns for aid. Our royal flagship and vice-flagship, in the meanwhile, were approaching so close in to her that the rest of the enemy's vessels gave signs of coming in to her assistance, and we made sure that at last we should be able to close with them, which was our only way of gaining the victory. At this moment the wind freshened in favour of the enemy's flagship, and we saw that she was getting away from us, and had no further need of the shallops that were towing her out. The enemy was then able to get to windward of us again. As the duke saw that further attack was useless, and that we were already off the Wight, he fired a signal gun and proceeded on the voyage, followed by the rest of the Armada in good order; the enemy remaining a long way astern.

'On this day the duke sent Captain Pedro de Leon to Dunkirk to advise the Duke of Parma as to his whereabouts and inform him of events, pressing him to come out with all possible speed and join the Armada.'

The captain of one of the Seville hulks witnessed the later stages of the engagement:

4 August: Battle for the Solent

'Off the Isle of Wight, we found the wind fair and were aweather of them, going very near of them and they flying. We had them broken and the victory three parts won, when the enemy's "*capitana* turned upon our armada, and the galleon *San Mateo*, which had the point of the weather wing gave way to it, retreating into the body of the Armada. Seeing that, the enemy took heart and turned with his whole fleet or the greater part of it, and charged upon the said wing, in such wise that we who were there were driven into a corner, so that if the duke had not gone about with his flagship, instead of conquerors that we were, we should have come out vanquished that day. Seeing that, those of his armada that had been cut off, bore up to rejoin.'

Howard, unsurprisingly, provided a rather different version of events:

'The next morning… there was a great galleon of the Spaniards short of her company to the southwards. They of Sir John Hawkins his squadron, being next, towed, and recovered so near that the boats were beaten off with musket shot; whereupon three of the galleasses and an armada issued out of the Spanish fleet, with whom the lord admiral in the *Ark* and the Lord Thomas Howard in the *Golden Lion*, fought a long time and much damaged them, that one of them was fain to be carried away upon the careen; and another, by a shot from the *Ark*, lost her lantern, which came swimming by, and the third his nose.

'At length it began to blow a little gale, and the Spanish fleet edged up to succour their galleasses, and so rescued them and the galleon, after which the galleasses were never seen in fight anymore, so bad was their entertainment in this encounter. Then the fleets drawing near one to another, there began some fight, but it continued not long, saving that the *Nonpareil* and the *Mary Rose* struck their topsails and lay awhile by the whole fleet of Spain very bravely, during which time the *Triumph*, to the northward of the Spanish fleet, was so far to leeward as, doubting that some of the Spanish army might weather her, she towed off with the help of sundry boats, and so recovered the wind. The *Bear* and the *Elizabeth Jonas*, perceiving her distress, bare with her for her rescue, and put themselves, through their hardiness, into like perils, but made their parties good notwithstanding, until they had recovered the wind; and so that day's fight ended, which was a very sharp fight for the time.'

Much of the significance of the day's action rests upon the question of whether or not the Spaniards actually intended to attempt the capture of the Isle of Wight. Many of the English certainly thought that they did, and congratulated themselves for having thwarted the plan. Yet the evidence remains unclear. None of the Spanish accounts actually say there was any such scheme, and given the nature of the debate in the Spanish council of war a few days before, when approaching Plymouth, it is perhaps unlikely that Medina Sidonia would later have deviated from his decision to follow the king's orders to head straight up-Channel and join Parma without attempting a landing on the way.

However, he had also been instructed to avoid seeking action with the English fleet. Already at Portland Bill, and again off the Isle of Wight, he had stretched his obedience of those orders to their utmost limits, and so it cannot be ruled out that he may have considered entering the Solent, though wisely omitting to mention the fact in his later report to Philip.

So far as the actual fighting of the day is concerned, the galleasses, despite English claims to the contrary, had proved quite effective in the calm conditions of the earlier part of the engagement. Given a little luck and a little more placidity in seafaring conditions, they might have crippled – and perhaps even captured – Frobisher's *Triumph*. While this would not, of course, have significantly weakened Howard's fleet, it would have been a serious blow to English morale, and a major boost for the Spaniards.

However, the Spaniards' claim to have had the better of the day's fighting needs to be treated with caution. Overall, the result seems to have been a repetition of the previous encounters, with the English avoiding Spanish attempts to board them, while firing from too great a distance to do serious damage. But it does appear that the fighting had been the fiercest of the campaign to date. In the three engagements so far, the Spaniards admitted to losing a total of 167 dead and 241 wounded. It was, however, customary for commanders to under-report their casualty figures, in order to continue claiming 'dead men's pay' for their own benefit: so it is possible that actual losses were considerably higher. English losses for the same period are unknown, but were relatively light.

More significantly, with the decisive action of the campaign still likely to lie ahead, both Howard and Medina Sidonia were seriously concerned about the amounts of powder and shot they had expended. Both had urgently sent for new supplies, with Howard far more likely than Medina Sidonia to receive them. This, and the lack of news from Parma, had to be major concerns for the latter, as he continued his voyage up-Channel. For both commanders there was still everything to fight for.

Friday 5 August: A Waiting Game

Wind and Weather: wind drops before dawn; at sunset light breeze, probably from the west; sea calm

Neither side was anxious to renew battle. Both were concerned about ammunition shortages; Medina Sidonia, with his overall strategy apparently still succeeding, was intent upon making contact with Parma as soon as possible, while Howard wanted to avoid battle until he had been resupplied and was reinforced by Seymour's squadron. Throughout the day, both fleets moved on slowly eastwards at about one knot in the near calm.

Possibly on this same day Howard had written to the queen, warning her that if he did not receive substantial new supplies of powder and shot, he would be forced to 'forbear to assail and stand upon his guard until he shall be furnished from hence.' Sir Francis Walsingham responded by ordering that 'twenty-three last of powder and… proportion of bullet accordingly' be sent post haste to the English fleet.

As on previous days, Howard was joined by a steady stream of small ships, mostly bringing the much-needed powder and shot. Some also brought gentleman volunteers, eager to take part in the decisive action they felt to be imminent. Howard and his seasoned commanders were unenthusiastic about these newcomers, with the lord admiral eventually making clear that he did not require any more men, while most of the ships that joined him were too small to do anything other than present a 'show' for the Spaniards.

In the evening, Howard called a council of war, at which it was resolved not to engage the enemy again until the Straits of Dover were reached, and with good fortune, the Armada trapped between Howard and Seymour. Probably as a gesture of confidence after the indecisive outcome of the actions of the previous few days, Howard knighted John Hawkins, Martin Frobisher, and several of his captains, including Lord Thomas Howard, Lord Sheffield, Roger Townsend, and the remarkable octogenarian George Beeston, commander of the 400-ton *Dreadnought*.

Meanwhile, Medina Sidonia described his anxiety for news from Parma:

'Friday, the 5th, broke calm, both fleets being within sight of each other, and the duke sent another *felucca* to the Duke of Parma with the pilot Domingo Ochoa on-board, to beg him to send us some cannon balls of 4, 5, and 10 pounds as a great many had been spent in the skirmishing of the last few days. He was also instructed to request Parma to send out forty flyboats immediately to join the Armada; and so by their aid to enable us to come to close quarters with the enemy, which we had hitherto found it quite impossible to do, in consequence of our vessels being very heavy in comparison with the lightness of the enemy's ships. Ochoa was also instructed to press upon the Duke of Parma the necessity of his being ready to come out and join the Armada the very day it came in sight of Dunkirk. The duke was very anxious on this point, as he feared Parma was not at Dunkirk; Don Rodrigo Tello not having returned, and no messenger having come from Parma. At sunset a breeze sprang up and the Armada got under way on the voyage towards Calais.'

In his own account, Howard emphasised how much his shortage of ammunition was hindering his operations:

'Now, forasmuch as our powder and shot was well wasted, the lord admiral thought it was not good in policy to assail them any more until their coming near unto Dover, where he should find the army which he had left under the conduction of the Lord Henry Seymour and Sir William Wynter, knight, ready to join with his lordship, whereby our fleet should be much strengthened, and in the meantime, better store of munitions might be provided from the shore. On Friday… his lordship, as well in reward of their good services in these former fights, as also for the encouragement of the rest, called the Lord Thomas Howard, the Lord Sheffield, Sir Roger Townsend, Sir Martin Frobisher and Sir John Hawkins, and gave them all the order of knighthood aboard the *Ark*. All this day and Saturday … the Spaniards went always before the English army like sheep, during which time the justices of the peace near the seacoast, the Earl of Sussex, Sir George Carey, and the captains of the forts and castles along the coast, sent us men, powder, shot, victuals and ships to aid and assist us.'

Saturday 6 August: Where is Parma?

Wind and Weather: SW wind with heavy showers; sea slight with poor visibility

During Friday evening the wind had freshened from the west, and continued to increase during the night, so that Saturday morning found the English and Spanish fleets – scarcely a mile apart – heading rapidly towards the Straits of Dover.

Medina Sidonia now had a difficult decision to make. He had still heard nothing from Parma, and was beginning to doubt if the commander of the Army of Flanders would in fact be ready to join him. But the king's orders gave him little leeway, and no clear course of action if the planned rendezvous did not take place, other than the suggestion that Medina Sidonia might then seize a base such as the Isle of Wight. There was, in fact, no possibility – even if the wind

6 August: Where is Parma?

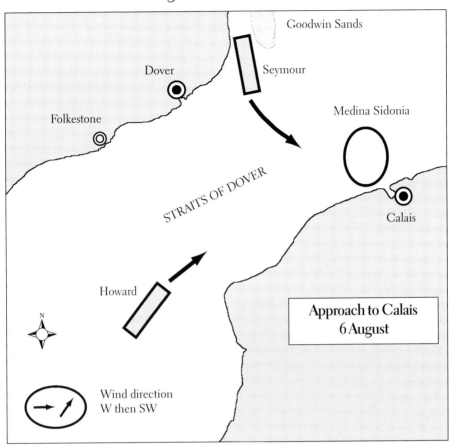

Goodwin Sands

Dover

Seymour

Medina Sidonia

Folkestone

STRAITS OF DOVER

Calais

Howard

**Approach to Calais
6 August**

N

Wind direction
W then SW

changed and gave the Spaniards the weather-gauge again – that the Armada would be able to fight its way back westwards, attacked by Howard in front and Seymour in the rear. Furthermore, Medina Sidonia's pilots warned him that unless he anchored in the Straits of Dover, with Calais Roads the only realistic location, the currents were such that the Armada would be swept out into the North Sea with no real prospect of putting about to rendezvous with Parma.

As Medina Sidonia himself admitted, there was a good deal of opposition amongst his senior commanders to the decision to anchor, but they can only have proposed one of two alternatives: either they were hoping for a favourable wind in which to bring the English fleet to battle, or – having had ample opportunity to get the measure of their opponents in the skirmishes of the preceding days – they wanted to abandon the whole enterprise and head back to Spain. The army commander, Francisco de Bobadilla, was clearly one of those who opposed halting at Calais, later writing angrily that 'I do not know whose idea it was that in a port with such strong cross currents and on an open shore

Navigation

By the middle of the sixteenth century the Spanish and Portuguese were the acknowledged experts in oceanic navigation, possessing the largest number of skilled pilots and deep sea navigators. Navigation, when out of sight of land, mainly depended upon calculations based upon noon sightings of the sun, with the aid of instruments known as astrolabes or cross staffs and mathematical tables, which would enable the ship's latitude to be found. It would not be possible to calculate longitude for a further two centuries. Calculations could also be made with the aid of the Pole Star, though if the weather was too thick to allow sightings, then a ship's position could only be estimated by means of a compass and 'dead-reckoning', an inaccurate process.

The Armada anticipated little difficulty in navigating, as most of its voyage was intended to take place in coastal waters, with land frequently in sight, enabling pilots to give an accurate position through the use of sounding leads and pilot books.

The disaster that eventually overwhelmed so many Armada ships off Ireland was the result of desperation forcing them into uncharted coastal waters rather than poor navigation as such.

with cross winds and so many shoals from one side to the other these forces could join, for it is not a port in which one could delay without danger.'

So at about 4.00 pm, as the Armada came into the offshore anchorage of Calais Roads, the Spaniards, obeying a pre-arranged signal, and showing excellent discipline, simultaneously dropped anchor, 4 miles from Calais, and 24 miles from Parma's presumed main port of embarkation at Dunkirk. The Spaniards possibly hoped that they would surprise the English with this sudden move, and cause Howard's fleet to be swept past the Armada into the North Sea, so losing the weather-gauge. But Howard and his commanders were well-prepared, and almost simultaneously with the Armada, the English ships also dropped anchor, in Whitsand Bay, lying within 'long culverin shot' of the enemy.

Late in the afternoon the Spaniards sighted Seymour's squadron – which they believed to be commanded by Hawkins – coming up from the north-east to join Howard. The English fleet now totalled an estimated 140 sail, including some thirty Queen's Ships and numerous armed merchant ships, of which, one Spaniard ruefully admitted: 'the worst, without their main-course or top sails, can beat the best sailors we have.' The Spaniards were also somewhat alarmed at the size of the united English fleet. Captain Estrade paid reluctant tribute to his opponents' ability: 'So this day, with such ships as came unto them along the coast there were above 150 sail, yet in that which I did see and others likewise there were but eighteen good galleons, or twenty, of 300 tons, and the rest small, which did amaze me. The English did well to accomplish their business (but with the secrets of God).'

The fortress and harbour of Calais, for so long an English possession, was now held for King Henry III of France. While officially neutral, the governor of Calais, Monsieur de Gourdan, had lost a leg while fighting the English, and his natural hostility towards his old enemies made him inclined to stretch his neutrality as much as he dared to the Spaniards' advantage. When Medina Sidonia sent some officers ashore to assure the governor of the Armada's peaceful intentions, Gourdan, while obeying the letter of the law in refusing to provide them with supplies, quietly told Medina Sidonia's representatives that there would be no objection to their purchasing them privately. He also warned them that the Armada's present anchorage was an unsafe one, because of strong currents and tides.

This was further unwelcome news for Medina Sidonia, who was, with increasing desperation, still awaiting word from Parma. That evening, he sent another, almost frantic, message to the duke: 'I am anchored here 2 leagues from Calais with the enemy's fleet on my flanks. They can cannonade me whenever they like and I shall be unable to do them much harm. If you can send me forty or fifty flyboats of your fleet I can, with their help, defend myself until you are ready to come out.' Medina Sidonia never more clearly demonstrated the weakness of the Spanish plan, or the mutual lack of understanding among its principal executioners. The intention had been that the Armada should provide protection for Parma's invasion flotilla, but Medina Sidonia was now, in effect, asking that Parma should defend him! But it would be next day before Medina Sidonia fully understood the true situation.

For the English commanders, although they had greater knowledge of the problems facing Parma, there could be no relaxation. Despite Howard's best efforts, the Armada had arrived at Calais both formidable and substantially intact. Although Howard was probably reassured by Seymour that a sortie by the invasion flotilla was likely to be fraught with difficulties, it could not be ruled out, while the danger from the Armada itself, which might easily launch its own assault on some English port, was as great as ever.

Seymour's vice admiral, Sir William Wynter, went to consult with Howard and put forward his own proposal to break the Spanish formation: 'Immediately, so soon as my lord admiral's ship was come to an anchor, he sent his pinnace aboard my ship for me, commanding me to come aboard his lordship, which I did; and having viewed myself the great hugeness of the Spanish army, did consider that it was not possible to remove them but by a device of firing of ships. His lordship did like very well of it, and said the next day he would call a council and put the same in practice.'

As night fell, both sides were anxiously awaiting the developments the next day was likely to bring. Many of the Spaniards were already full of foreboding regarding what the enemy might do. Don Luis Miranda, on Medina Sidonia's staff, was one of them: 'We rode there all night at anchor, with the enemy half a league from us, being resolved to wait, since there was nothing else to be done, and with a great presentment of evil from that devilish people and their arts.'

Medina Sidonia summarised the events of the day:

'At daybreak on Saturday, 6th, the fleets were close together, and sailed on without exchanging shots until ten o'clock in the day, our armada having the wind astern and the rearguard well up, in good order. At this hour the coast of France was sighted near Boulogne and we proceeded on our voyage to Calais Roads, where we arrived at four o'clock in the afternoon. There was some difference of opinion as to whether we should anchor here, the majority being in favour of sailing on. The duke, however, was informed by his pilots that if he proceeded any further the currents would force him to run out of the Channel into Norwegian waters, and he consequently decided to anchor off Calais, 7 leagues from Dunkirk, where Parma might join him. At five o'clock the order to drop anchor was given to the whole armada, and Captain Heredia was sent to visit the governor of Calais, M. de Gourdan, to explain the reason why we had anchored there and offer him friendship.

'This afternoon the enemy's fleet was reinforced by thirty-six sail, including five great galleons. This was understood to be John Hawkins' squadron, which had been watching Dunkirk, and the whole of the English fleet now anchored a league distant from our armada. Captain Heredia returned that night from Calais, bringing friendly assurances and promises of service from the governor. The duke despatched Secretary Arceo to Parma, to inform him of the position of the Armada, and to say that it was impossible for it to remain where it was without very great risk.'

Howard's report of the day's proceedings is notably terse:

'On Saturday, in the evening, the Spanish fleet came near unto Calais on the coast of Picardy, and there suddenly came to an anchor over against betwixt Calais and Scales Cleeves [Calais Cliffs] and our English fleet anchored short of them within culverin shot of the enemy.'

7 August: Waiting for Parma

Also on the scene was Captain Richard Thomas of the *Margaret and John*:

'We kept the wind of them, which is a very great advantage and special safety for the weaker part. By that means, to the great annoyance of our enemies, we have so daily pursued them at the heels, that they never had leisure to stop at any place along our English coast, until they came within 2 miles of Calais, where in the evening, very politicly, they came all upon a sudden to an anchor, purposing that our ships with the flood tide should be driven to leeward of them; but in happy time it was soon espied, and prevented by bringing our fleet to an anchor also in the wind of them.'

Sunday 7 August: Waiting for Parma

Wind and Weather: calm until about 5.00 am, then SW or SSW wind freshening with showers; wind probably veered later to N and NW

For Medina Sidonia this was the decisive day of the campaign. He felt he had fulfilled his orders, and brought his armada successfully to a suitable rendezvous-point with the Army of Flanders. Now it was for Parma to play his part. As the hours passed, Medina Sidonia grew steadily more anxious. The news that eventually arrived was not encouraging. The first report came from the original messenger whom the duke had sent to Parma, Don Rodrigo Tello de Guzman. His report shattered Medina Sidonia's hopes. Parma, he said, was still at Bruges, forty miles from Dunkirk. At Dunkirk, Tello had found no invasion army and only a handful of canal barges without masts or guns. Parma had told Tello the remainder of his invasion fleet was still dispersed along the canals, though he had 5,000 men at Nieuport and 15,300 at Dunkirk, who could be embarked within six days. Tello, however, thought that a fortnight would be a more realistic timescale. In the evening, Medina Sidonia's secretary – who had been joined by the inspector-general of the Armada, Don Jorge Manrique – returned, also with the view that it would be fifteen days before Parma was ready to put to sea. The envoys probably did not reveal that they had a heated argument with Parma: at one point almost coming to blows with him.

This was appalling news for the commanders of the Armada. But was it in fact accurate? To answer that question, we need to go back to the beginning of August. Tello, despatched by Medina Sidonia on 31 July, had only reached Parma on 6 August, the same day as the messenger sent after the Isle of Wight action. However, Parma claimed he had learnt on 2 August, from another source, of the Armada's arrival off the Lizard, and had at once put his men on the alert. On the 6th they began moving to the invasion ports, and almost all were embarked within the next thirty-six hours.

It was also true that in the middle of July many English and Dutch observers

Campaign Chronicle

The Duke of Medina Sidonia. The only known portrait of Alonso Perez de Guzman (1550–1619), head of one of the wealthiest and most influential families in Spain and captain-general of the Armada.

were reporting that Parma had concentrated almost 100 ships, including twenty-six warships, some of over 150 tons, at Dunkirk, and around 200 boats, mainly barges, at Nieuport. On 14 July, the States of Zeeland had concluded that the ships were 'in such readiness they could sail in ten or twelve days.' On 7 August (or so he claimed later), Parma had written to Medina Sidonia assuring him he would be ready to put to sea within two days. Arceo admitted that Parma had prepared 1,500 quintals of powder and 5,000 shot ready to send out to the Armada, and had promised to expedite their delivery.

But other eyewitnesses supported the view of Medina Sidonia's staff. Don Juan Manrique de Lara, who commanded one of Parma's German regiments, which was to embark at Nieuport, reported later that: 'We found the ships unfinished and none of them contained a single piece of artillery or anything to eat.' Another, Alonso Vazquez, commenting on the unfinished state of some of

7 August: Waiting for Parma

Parma's ships, felt that: 'In my opinion, speaking as an eyewitness, it was rash to hazard such a powerful army in weak and defenceless vessels like those prepared by Parma.'

A subaltern with the Army of Flanders, Don Carlos Coloma, who was at Dunkirk during the critical days, later testified: 'Whatever its cause, it is certain – I saw it myself – that during this time the preparation of the fleet in Dunkirk proceeded very slowly, so that when it was necessary to embark the Spanish infantry, not even the flagship was ready to sail.' However, when Parma learnt the Armada was off Calais: 'He resolved to embark, notwithstanding all other considerations and all dangers. The sergeant majors of the *tercios* immediately distributed the embarkation orders, which were obeyed at once, albeit with much laughter among the soldiers, because many of them were required to embark in ships on which no shipwright or ship's carpenter had worked. They were without munitions, without provisions, without sails.'

In fact, the troops would have required very little immediate provision for the short Channel crossing, and plans had been made for supply ships to follow on. It also seems that reports of the unpreparedness of Parma's ships were exaggerated. Despite the obstacles presented by unwilling or hostile workers, and shortage of funds, the majority of the invasion fleet was seaworthy, and able to begin embarking the troops. Whether or not there were enough vessels to carry the entire invasion force in one 'wave' is more doubtful.

Thus far, the evidence on balance marginally seems to support Parma. What was still unclear, however, was whether it was feasible for the invasion fleet to join Medina Sidonia. Much of this would depend upon the Dutch.

Whatever his well-founded doubts regarding the feasibility of the operation, Parma had, throughout the spring and early summer, taken steps to confuse the Dutch rebels about his intentions. As a result in the middle of July only twenty-four Dutch ships were off Dunkirk and Nieuport, compared with over 250 stationed elsewhere. Lord Henry Seymour was somewhat dismissive of Dutch efforts, commenting that: 'I think they desire more to regard their own coast than ours.'

It is usually assumed the Dutch were maintaining a close blockade at the entrances to the invasion ports. This was not in fact the case, for as Alonso Vazquez explained: 'Whenever Parma wanted to join his two fleets [at Nieuport and Dunkirk] it would be easy for him to do so, because the seacoast was clear of enemy ships. They could not come inshore because of the guard mounted by the places that secured it, besides the many currents and sandbanks created by the tides in the entire North Sea.'

As a result, even the largest vessels of the invasion flotilla could ride securely at anchor off Dunkirk, protected from attack by a large sandbank, and the troops could also be safely embarked in the same area.

Medina Sidonia consistently claimed the invasion flotilla would only be able to leave port with the aid of a spring tide, but Parma himself reported that this need applied to only a few of his vessels: 'And even supposing this should happen and we could not use them, but could undertake the task with the rest, I have... never thought of waiting for the spring tides or holding back for a moment for this reason.'

It was unlikely that all of Parma's ships could have been got out of port on one tide. But even though this would have meant that those which left on the first tide would have to wait in the roadstead for the remainder to sail with the next tide, it did not necessarily follow that the Dutch could have seriously hindered them. Most of the Dutch ships off Flanders were small – the largest only displacing 300 tons – and were mostly regarded by the English as being too small to be of use.

On 8 August Justin of Nassau had only thirty-five ships in his blockading squadron, and the same day warned the States of Zeeland that he could not withstand the concentrated Spanish force without reinforcement. Nor had he been able to close off the invasion ports completely. Parma had fairly regularly been able to send out pinnaces in search of news of the Armada, and two of Medina Sidonia's ships were actually able to enter Dunkirk and leave again after picking up supplies.

It was by no means out of the question, therefore – despite all their difficulties, delays, and misunderstandings – that on 7 August Parma and Medina Sidonia would be able to unite their forces within the next thirty-six hours. There were at least three possibilities open to them. The first would be for the Armada to attempt to defeat or disorganise the English and Dutch fleets sufficiently to prevent them from interfering with Parma's crossing. This, of course, was easier in theory than in practice, but would conform with the opinions of those, like Recalde, and perhaps Medina Sidonia himself, who had been chafing under the restrictions placed upon them by King Philip. However, the earlier failures to bring the English fleet to a decisive action made this option fairly unlikely to bring success.

Secondly, Medina Sidonia could have remained in a secure anchorage until Parma reported himself ready to sail. Unfortunately, Calais did not provide such a haven, as, even if the Spaniards were to gain entry to Calais harbour proper – either by persuasion or force – it was not deep enough to hold the largest galleons and could be blockaded by Howard.

The third option was rather more promising. It should have been possible to send a detachment of the smaller and medium-sized warships from the Armada into the anchorage off Dunkirk and Nieuport. Spanish vessels had actually done this in 1558 during the war with France, so the possibility should have been known to Medina Sidonia and his commanders. Even more feasibly, the four galleasses, which had already made a marked impression on the English, could have been despatched to clear a route through the Dutch for Parma to join the main fleet.

But, if this course was suggested to him, Medina Sidonia was evidently unwilling to take the risk of dividing his fleet. He may have felt, with some justification, that if Parma did put to sea he would be attacked by Seymour once he had cleared the safety of the sandbanks.

Nevertheless, the possibility of the two Spanish commanders coordinating some feasible plan of operations – given a few hours grace to communicate – remained. Parma himself would always assert he could have completed his embarkation on the night of 8 August, and sallied out to meet Medina Sidonia that night and early on 9 August: 'My statement that we needed no more than three days to embark and be ready to sail forth was not made without justification.'

If the English were to thwart them, they probably only had a few hours in which to do so.

That afternoon, Howard called another council of war aboard *Ark Royal*. The densely packed Spanish fleet in its anchorage was clearly impervious to an English attack unless its formation could be broken up. The obvious way to attempt this was by use of fireships. Sir Francis Walsingham had already ordered some of these to be prepared at Dover, and Sir Henry Palmer, in *Antelope*, was despatched to collect them. However, they were unlikely to arrive until the following evening (Monday 9 August) and the English commanders felt unable to risk waiting for so long. They decided to launch their own attack that same night. Drake, in a burst of patriotism, offered one of his own vessels, the 200-ton *Bark Bond*, to be converted as a fireship, and Hawkins followed suit with one of his. Eight vessels in all, including also the *Bark Talbot* (200 tons), *Thomas Drake* (200 tons), *Bear Yonge* (140 tons), *Elizabeth of Lowestoft* (90 tons), *The Angel of Hampton* and an unknown vessel of 150 tons, were chosen, and hidden amidst the rest of the fleet, work on preparing them began.

The Spaniards had meanwhile passed an uneasy day. The governor of Calais had allowed Medina Sidonia to send men ashore to purchase fresh provisions, but judging by a number who took the opportunity to desert, morale in the Armada was in some cases already brittle. The fear of attack by fireships heightened Spanish fears. In the forefront of their minds was the incident during the Siege of Antwerp in 1588, when the Italian, Frederigo Gambelli, in the service of the Dutch rebels, had prepared a series of vessels filled with explosives – the notorious 'hell-burners' – and launched them to destroy a Spanish pontoon

Fireships and 'Hell-Burners'

The much-feared 'hell-burners' were a mixture of explosive and incendiary vessels designed by the Italian Frederigo Gambelli and employed at Antwerp in April 1585, against a large Spanish bridge of boats. Some were designed to explode by the use of a delayed action time fuse. Some were filled with powder and shot and designed to explode when the heat of the fires ignited the powder. Their use at Antwerp not only caused mass panic and chaos among the Spaniards, but also resulted in about 800 dead. The fear of a repetition of their use by the English was a major factor in the confusion that gripped the Spanish ships at Calais on 8 August 1588.

bridge with horrendous loss of life. Gambelli was known to be now in England, and the English, they feared, were about to launch the same weapon against them.

There were clearly laid-down procedures for countering an attack by fireships. Medina Sidonia ordered a number of pinnaces to be prepared, carrying grapnels and long poles to haul or push the fireships clear, and anchored them in a defensive perimeter around the seaward flank of the Armada. The rest of the fleet was to remain at anchor while the pinnaces tackled the threat. Only if some of the fireships got through were they to slip their anchors (buoying them for later recovery), stand out to sea until the fireships burnt themselves out, and then to return to their anchorage again.

Amid rising tension, at about 4.00 pm, an English pinnace was sighted approaching the Armada and shots were exchanged. This vessel was probably despatched to obtain up-to-date information on the Armada's position.

As darkness fell, the Spaniards waited the night's events with mounting dread. The Duke of Parma justified his state of readiness:

'The men who have recently come here from the duke seeing the boats unarmed and with no artillery on-board and the men not shipping have been trying to claim that we are not ready. They are mistaken. The boats are, and have been for months, in proper order for the work they have to do, namely to take the men across. We have not as many seamen as we ought to have; but enough for the job. The boats are so small that the troops cannot be kept on-board for long. There is no room to turn around, and they would certainly fall ill, rot and die. Putting the men on-board these low, small boats can be done in a very short time, and I am confident in this respect there will be no shortcoming in Your Majesty's service.'

Medina Sidonia took a different view:

'On Sunday, the 7th, at daybreak, Captain Don Rodrigo Tello arrived from Dunkirk and reported that the Duke of Parma was at Bruges, where he had visited him, and although he had expressed great joy at the arrival of the Armada, he had not come to Dunkirk up to the night of Saturday, the 6th, when Tello had left there, nor had the embarkation of the men and stores been commenced.

'On Sunday morning the governor of Calais sent his nephew to visit the duke bringing with him a great present of fresh provisions. He informed the duke that the place where he was lying was extremely dangerous to stay in, in consequence of the cross currents of the Channel being very strong. In view of the friendly attitude of the governor, the duke sent the Provedore Bernage de Pedroso, with the paymaster, to purchase provisions. He also sent at night Don Jorge Manrique to Parma, to urge upon him to expedite his coming out.'

Though no fighting had taken place, Sunday 7 August was one of the decisive days of the campaign. The full consequences of the lack of understanding of each other's difficulties, which had dogged Parma and Medina Sidonia since planning for the invasion of England had begun, was now clearly apparent. Though both men would blame the other for the debacle, the situation was not, in fact, irretrievable. Given a day or two's grace, the invasion attempt was still possible. All depended upon whether the English would grant them that time.

For Howard and his officers the situation that evening was not necessarily desperate, but certainly critical. There could be no guarantee the attack by fireships would succeed. If it failed, they faced the prospect of having to tackle the combined forces of Parma and Medina Sidonia. Given the fighting so far, while the English fleet could reasonably hope for success, it was by no means certain. That night the entire fate of the campaign hung in the balance.

Monday 8 August, Midnight–6.00 am: The Hell-Burners of Calais

Wind and Weather: wind SSE; sea calm

Under cover of darkness, and hidden in the midst of the English fleet, the fireships were prepared. Stripped of most of their equipment, they were then filled with combustible material of all kinds, including sails, spars, timber, and sacking, all smothered in pitch, tar and oil. More pitch and oil were applied to their masts and rigging. The guns were in many cases double-shotted, so that their explosions would add to enemy alarm. Manned by skeleton crews, equipped

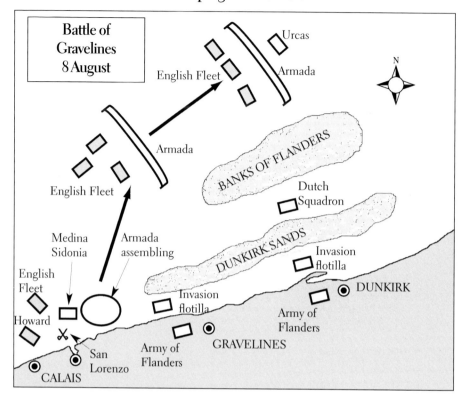

to light the network of slow match that covered each craft, every vessel towing a boat on which the men would escape, the fireships began to slip quietly towards the Armada.

The attackers were assisted by the freshening wind and a high spring tide, but the alarm was raised at about midnight, when two of the ships were apparently fired prematurely. 'Two fires were seen kindled in the English fleet, which increased to eight; and suddenly eight ships with all sail set and fair wind and tide, came straight toward our *capitana* and the rest of the fleet, all burning fiercely.' They would reach the Spaniards in about fifteen to twenty minutes.

Medina Sidonia's pinnaces and other small craft went into action, and managed to grapple and pull ashore two of the attackers. But, aided by the wind and tide, the remainder continued to bear down on the Armada, their double-shotted guns exploding as they did so. Logically, they might have been expected to fail. Calais Roads were wide, giving plenty of space for manoeuvre and evasion, and it would soon have become apparent that the fireships were not in fact the dreaded 'hell-burners', were too few in number, and contained no explosives. However, against the odds, they succeeded.

According to one angry Spaniard:

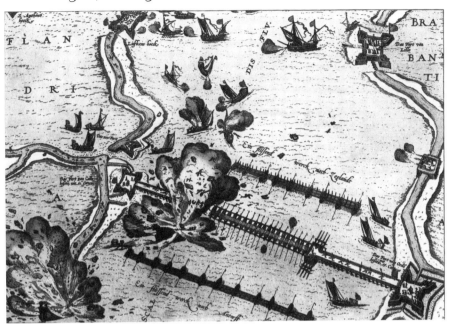

The 'Hell-Burners' of Antwerp.

'Fortune so favoured the English, that there grew from this piece of industry just what they counted on, for they dislodged us with eight vessels, an exploit which with 130 they had not been able nor dared to attempt. When the morning came they had gained the weather-gauge of us, for we found ourselves scattered in every direction.'

It is usually claimed the spectacle of the approaching flames caused panic among the ships of the Armada, but the English seem to have exaggerated their effects. Though one Spanish eyewitness hints at the alarm that had seized some of the crews of the Armada:

'The eight ships, filled with artificial fire and ordnance, advanced in line at a distance of a couple of pike's lengths between them. But by God's grace, before they arrived, while they were yet between the two fleets, one of them flared up with such fierceness and great noise as were frightful, and at this the ships of the Armada cut their cables at once, leaving their anchors, spreading their sails, and running out to sea; and the whole eight fireships went drifting between the fleet and the shore with the most terrible flames that may be imagined.'

Campaign Chronicle

Fireships in action.

Most of the Spanish crews seem to have managed, despite the darkness and confusion, the difficult feat of setting sail and cutting their cables, the only apparent casualty being the *San Lorenzo*, flagship of the galleasses, which in the confusion collided with another galleass, the *Girona*, then with de Leiva's *Rata Encoronada*, damaging her rudder.

With the fireships now burning themselves out harmlessly on the shore, Medina Sidonia's plan had been for the Armada to re-form, recover its anchors and resume its previous moorings. That this did not happen was the result of several factors. The darkness, the wind, the strong currents, and the spring tide carrying them towards the North Sea made it virtually impossible for the Armada to return as planned. It also seems highly likely that some of those commanders who had all along been opposed to the halt at Calais made little effort to obey the duke's orders.

The outcome was a major – and perhaps unexpected – English success. Unable, owing to the strong spring tide, to return to their original anchorage and pick up what were in most cases their best anchors, the Spanish ships found that their remaining ones were unable to grip in a seabed that provided poor holding, and they drifted north-east, in the direction of Gravelines and the Banks of Flanders. The Armada had not only lost the tight formation it had maintained for most of the past week, but it had now irretrievably lost any chance of linking up with Parma and the Army of Flanders. As dawn would reveal, Medina Sidonia's situation was increasingly desperate.

And yet Medina Sidonia was still recovering from the panic caused by the appearance of fireships. His subsequent report reveals a fear of 'fire machines' and exploding mines:

'At midnight two fires were perceived on the English fleet, and these two gradually increased to eight. They were eight vessels with sails set, which were drifting with the current directly towards our flagship and the rest of the Armada, all of them burning with great fury. When the duke saw them approaching, and that our men had not diverted them, he, fearing that they might contain fire machines or mines, ordered the flagship to let go the cables, the rest of the Armada receiving similar orders, with an intimation that when the fires had passed they were to return to the same positions again. The leading galleass, in trying to avoid a ship, ran foul of the *San Juan de Sicilia*, and became so crippled that she was obliged to drift ashore. The current was so strong that although the flagship, and some of the vessels near her, came to anchor and fired off a signal gun, the other ships of the Armada did not perceive it, and were carried by the current towards Dunkirk.'

Meanwhile, from the deck of his ship, *Vanguard*, Vice Admiral Sir William Wynter, their original proposer, keenly watched the effects of the fireships:

'about twelve of the clock that night six ships were brought and prepared with a saker shot, and going in a front, having the wind and tide with them, and their ordnance being charged, were fired; and the men that were the executers, so soon as the fire was made, they did abandon the ships, and entered into five boats that were appointed for the saving of them. This matter did put such terror among the Spanish army that they were fain to let slip their cables and anchors; and did work, as it did appear, great mischief among them by reason of the suddenness of it. We might perceive that there were two great fires more than ours, and far greater and huger than any of our vessels that we fired could make.'

But not all of the English were unreservedly delighted at the success of the fireships. Captain Henry Whyte, whose ship the *Bark Talbot*, was one of those employed, was rather more concerned about compensation:

'There [at Calais] it was resolved to put them from their anchor, and ships were allotted to the fire to perform the enterprise; among the rest, the ship

Campaign Chronicle

I had in charge, the *Bark Talbot*, was one; so that now I rest like one that had his house burnt, and one of these days I must come to your honour for permission to go a-begging.'

Monday 8 August, 6.00 am–Midnight: The Battle of Gravelines

Wind and Weather: wind in morning from the SSW, eventually freshening from the NW by evening; sea very rough with WNW wind

The arrival of dawn brought the eagerly watching English the sight they had so long dreamt of. Much of the Armada lay scattered over a wide area running north-eastwards beyond Gravelines, towards the Flanders Banks of the North Sea. But about 1 mile to the north of the English fleet, Medina Sidonia's *San Martin* had succeeded in anchoring, and firing off a signal gun, had managed to gather around her some of the stalwarts of the fighting of the previous week, including Recalde's *San Juan*, the Portuguese galleons, *San Marcos* and *San Mateo*, and either the *San Felipe* or Oquendo's *Santa Ana*. This core of veterans repre-sented a possible rallying point for the remainder of the Armada, and as the English fleet up-anchored to the sound of trumpets, it would have seemed that Howard's priority should be to destroy or scatter them. Indeed, Lord Henry Seymour said as much, explaining that it 'had been resolved the day before My lord admiral should give the first charge, Sir Francis Drake the next, and myself the third; it fell out that the galleass distressed, altered My Lord's former

On board Howard's flagship: a Victorian reconstruction.

determination, as I suppose, by prosecuting the destruction of her.'

For also in sight, probably still attempting to limp towards the safety of Calais Harbour, was Hugo de Moncada's *capitana*, the *San Lorenzo*. The galleasses had been in the forefront of much of the Channel fighting, and were regarded as formidable adversaries. But while it was undoubtedly tempting to seize the opportunity to finish one of them off, it would hardly have seemed to be a priority for Howard himself. However, leaving the remainder of the fleet to go after Medina Sidonia and his little force, the lord admiral led his own squadron in pursuit of *San Lorenzo*.

Possibly panicked by the sight of the approaching English ships, Moncada's galleass now ran aground just short of Calais Harbour, tilting far over on its side.

Approaching the stricken Spaniard as closely as he could, Howard ordered ships' boats filled with boarding parties to be launched to capture her. *Ark Royal's* own longboat, packed with sixty soldiers under Lieutenant Amyas Preston, was first to get alongside, followed by longboats from the *Margaret and John*, which in her eagerness for a share of the spoil had also run aground. The attackers were, in theory, considerably outnumbered, but as one Spaniard explained, so many of the crew jumped overboard and swam for the shore that: 'not more than fifty men stood by the captain to defend the ship.' However, the English discovered that the steep canting side of the *San Lorenzo* was frustrating their attempts to board, and for the next half hour a hot skirmish continued between opposing musketeers, which cost the English a number of casualties, including Lieutenant Preston. The attackers were preparing to withdraw in frustration, when a lucky musket shot hit Moncada squarely between the eyes, killing him instantly.

Some of the crew of *San Lorenzo* had already begun to wade through the shallows to the safety of Calais, and with Moncada's fall resistance crumbled: 'They put up two handkerchiefs upon two rapiers signifying that they desired truce... Many there were slain by the sword, others leaped overboard by heaps on the other side and fled to the shore, swimming and wading. Some escaped with being wet, some, and that were many, were drowned.' The English scrambled aboard and set to work looting, with Lieutenant Richard Tomson and his men from the *Margaret and John* in the forefront. Monsieur De Gourdan, the governor of Calais, sent emissaries to inform the English that while he had no objection to their looting the *San Lorenzo*, the ship herself, with her guns, belonged to him. Some of the English sailors made the mistake of robbing the French messengers, and as a result the English boats came under fire from the guns of Calais Castle. The boarding parties withdrew, with the *Margaret and John*, still aground, being holed twice before the rising tide eventually floated her off. The English had carried off about 20,000 ducats and fourteen chests containing other valuables. But they had suffered more casualties in the attack on *San Lorenzo*

Close-quarter fighting: a Victorian impression. Note the swivel gun, and the short-barrelled calivers. It is unlikely that archers were employed by either side.

8 August, 6.00 am–Midnight: The Battle of Gravelines

– including twenty drowned in their hasty departure – than in the whole of the rest of the campaign.

While Howard had been amusing himself in this arguably irresponsible fashion for up to two hours, and significantly reducing the odds against Medina Sidonia, fierce fighting had begun out to sea.

The Battle of Gravelines is frustratingly poorly documented, so the exact course of events is unclear. Drake's, Hawkins', and Frobisher's squadrons went in pursuit of the Armada, and quickly became engaged with *San Martin* and her consorts. For a time Medina Sidonia's flagship seems to have been surrounded by opponents, with Captain Vanegas estimating that at one point she had seventeen English ships to port and seven to starboard.

Medina Sidonia, understandably bitter at what he saw as deliberate desertion by some of his captains, was engaged in a fight for time for the Armada to re-form. Pinnaces had been sent at dawn to round up the scattered ships, but neither their task – nor any clear understanding of the sequence of events – was assisted by heavy seas and bad weather: which remained blustery all day, with poor visibility, often down to a few hundred yards.

The initial fighting centred around Medina Sidonia and his squadron of about half a dozen ships. In all probability, no more than about thirty or forty of the larger English ships actually took part in the fighting, and rather fewer on the Spanish side. It is unclear what role, if any (other than as spectators), the 100 or so smaller English vessels had. The bulk of the Armada, meanwhile, was scattered about seven miles off Gravelines when the action began, with the main fighting commencing further west and shifting between Calais and Dunkirk for most of the day, while the Armada gradually resumed its old formation.

This time, learning from their failures in the earlier skirmishes, the English were determined to make every shot count, and closed to a range of 100 yards or less. Medina Sidonia claimed the English 'had the advantage of artillery, we only in the fire of muskets and arquebuses'. The first onslaught on Medina Sidonia was made by Drake's squadron, his own *Revenge* taking the lead. The English followed their usual tactics of firing their bow guns as they approached, then luffing up (turning into the wind) to bring their broadsides to bear before swinging back downwind in order to reload out of range. Though neither side's fire was particularly rapid, the Spaniards were as ever hindered by their gunnery techniques, which were probably made even more ineffective by the heavy seas. Although Captain Vengas claimed that *San Martin* had fired 300 rounds from her forty-eight guns in the course of an action that probably lasted for about six hours, this amounted to barely one round per gun per hour. Even so, the English ships did not escape unscathed: *Revenge* was 'pierced through by cannon balls of all sizes above forty times'. Virtually all of these were fired by *San Martin*. One rather unlikely account claimed Drake's cabin was 'twice shot through', and that the bed of a gentleman 'was taken quite from under him with the force of a bullet', though quite why the gentleman should have been taking his ease in the midst of the battle is not explained.

San Martin herself, for a long time fighting unsupported, suffered severe damage. Vanegas claimed that she was hit a total of 107 times, in hull, masts, and sails. She was holed several times below the waterline, causing serious leaks, which her divers struggled to plug, while one 50-pound shot was said to have gone clean through her hull at one side and out of the other, despite the hull being seven planks thick.

Initially, the only real support Medina Sidonia seems to have received was from the Marquis of Pimentel's *San Marcos*, which took off some of the pressure as Drake sheered off, possibly to attack the re-forming vessels to the north, although sources are silent regarding his actions for the remainder of the day. Sir Martin Frobisher, predictably, was scathing about Drake's performance: 'Sir Francis Drake reports that no man hath done any good service but he; but he shall well understand that others have done as good service, as he and better. He came bragging up at the first, indeed, and gave them his prow and his broadside, and then kept his luff and was glad that he was gone again like a cowardly knave or a traitor. I rest doubtful, but the one I will swear.'

But Medina Sidonia was given no respite. He now came under attack from Thomas Fenner, in the *Nonpareil*, followed by at least twenty other ships: probably part of Drake's squadron. Fenner was quickly followed by Frobisher, who engaged the *San Martin* at pistol range, keeping just far enough away to avoid being grappled. Other ships of his squadron followed Frobisher's example, causing further damage to *San Martin*'s bows, stern, and sides.

It was now the turn of Hawkins' squadron, headed by his flagship, *Victory*, to continue Medina Sidonia's ordeal. By now the *San Martin*'s starboard side, with her rigging and sails, had been heavily damaged and her decks were strewn with casualties. Pedro de Calderon wrote that: 'The holes made in her hull between wind and water caused so great a leakage that two divers could hardly stop them up with hemp caulking and lead plates, working all day.'

A priest, Friar Bernardo de Gongora, who was aboard the *San Martin*, was stunned by the impact of battle:

'It was the greatest war and confusion that there has been in the world, in respect of the great amount of fire and smoke and of there being ships on the shore of Flanders. There were many ships which went on fighting in eight cubits of water. And all this day we had been holding ourselves with the bowline held against the weather so as not to run aground on the banks, and thus our ships could not ply their artillery as they wished. Some of the people died in our ship but none of quality, and it was a miracle that the duke escaped.'

San Martin's trial lasted for about two hours, during which she and her companions continued to drift slowly northwards towards the remainder of the Armada, which, in an act of remarkable – though little-appreciated leadership – de Leiva had managed to rally and put back into something like its old formation.

It was de Leiva who, at about 10.00 am, led the main fighting ships of the Armada to support Medina Sidonia in a battle of growing intensity. With him and his *Rata Encoronada* came Recalde and his *San Juan,* accompanied by the remainder of the Portuguese galleons. Oquendo in *Santa Ana* was joined by the Castilian galleons *San Juan* and the *San Juan de Sicilia* of Don Diego Tellez Enriques.

Ferocious fighting, at the closest range of the campaign so far, now began. Then Seymour's ships entered the fight on the English side, as Sir William Wynter explained, holding their fire 'until we came within six score paces of them.' Seymour's assault seems to have been directed against the starboard wing of the still re-forming Armada, and broke into it, causing four Spanish ships to collide. As they attempted to disentangle themselves, Seymour's ships poured in their broadsides at close range, attempting to isolate stragglers.

At one point, the galleon *San Felipe* was surrounded by no less than seventeen English ships, whose fire damaged her rudder, brought down her foremast, and inflicted 200 casualties among her crew. Her commander, Don Francisco de Toledo, tried to grapple the English ship nearest to him, which evaded the attempt, and 'assaulted him and by shooting of ordnance brought him to great extremity.' Toledo challenged his tormentors to hand-to-hand combat, but in reply was summoned to surrender by:

'one Englishman standing in the maintop with his sword and buckler [who] called out "Good soldiers that you are, surrender to the fair terms we offer you." The only answer he got was a gunshot which brought him down in the sight of everyone. And the cannonier then ordered the muskets and arquebusiers into action. The enemy [probably the *Rainbow* of Seymour's squadron] thereupon retired, while our men shouted out that they were cowards, abusing them for want of spirit, calling them Lutheran chickens, and desiring them to return to the fight.'

The *San Felipe* was rescued by the Portuguese galleons *San Mateo* and *San Luis,* which in turn became heavily engaged, along with Don Alonso de Luzon's

Valencera and the *Begoña* of the Indian Guard. All suffered heavy damage, but in particular the *San Mateo*, which came under close-range attack from Wynter's *Vanguard* and Seymour's *Rainbow*. The latter came so close that one over-excited Englishman leapt aboard *San Mateo*, where he was promptly 'cut to bits'.

But the English gunners had inflicted massive damage on the *San Mateo*, whose commander, Pimentel, was thought by some to have deliberately flung his ship into the thickest of the action to compensate for what was seen as his poor performance in the action off the Isle of Wight. She was 'a thing of pity to see, riddled with shot like a sieve… in a sinking condition, the pumps were powerless to diminish the water, all her sails and rigging were torn and sorely destroyed; of her sailors many perished, and of her soldiers few were left.'

While the fight to save the *San Mateo* continued, it was the turn of the *Begoña* and *San Juan de Sicilia* to come under a hail of fire, as they made perhaps the most determined attempt of the day to board some of their tormentors. They 'came near to boarding the enemy, yet could they not grapple with them, they fighting with their great ordnance our men defending themselves with harquebus fire and musket, the range being very small.'

As this account suggests, in some cases the Spanish ships bearing the brunt of the action were now running out of ammunition for their heavier guns. It seems that Parma's promised supplies had not arrived in time, and although there were significant amounts of heavy shot available in some of the store ships, little of this seems to have been transferred to replenish the stocks of the fighting ships during the halt at Calais. As a result, some of Medina Sidonia's finest ships could only endure the enemy fire in silence. One such seems to have been Martin de Bertendona's *Regazona*, which was seen wallowing in the increasingly heavy seas, her guns silent, with bloodstained water sloshing over board and only her arque-busiers maintaining a semblance of resistance.

Sir William Wynter estimated that his squadron fired some 500 demi-cannon and demi-culverin shots at the enemy, all within at least musket range.

By now it was becoming clear that some of the battered Spanish ships were doomed. On the stricken *San Mateo*, Pimental begged Medina Sidonia, whose own flagship was sorely battered, to send him one of his divers. Despite his own problems, the duke did so, but it was obvious that *San Mateo* was doomed. She gradually fell astern, and eventually was beached between Ostend and Sluys. Now it was the turn of Justin of Nassau's Dutch blockaders, who swarmed aboard the stricken Spaniard. The men of the *San Mateo*, knowing their likely fate, resisted desperately for two hours. Then Pimentel, probably having exhausted his ammunition, asked for terms. He and some of his officers were saved for ran-soming, but most of their men were 'cast overboard and slain.'

The *San Felipe* was probably the next to succumb. She was secured alongside

8 August, 6.00 am–Midnight: The Battle of Gravelines

The Battle of Gravelines.

the *urca, Doncella*, in order that her crew could be evacuated. But *Doncella* herself was apparently near to sinking, and *San Felipe*'s captain, Juan Poza de Santiso, and Maestre de Campo Francisco de Toledo returned to their own ship, saying it would be better to die in a galleon than in a hulk. As it happened, *Doncella* did not sink, but the *San Felipe* drifted ashore between Nieuport and Ostend. Her crew were slightly luckier than the men of the *San Mateo*. Pinnaces despatched by Parma rescued some of them, including their commanders. Justin of Nassau's men attempted to salvage *San Felipe*, and floated her off, but she sank before she could be got into the port of Flushing.

At least one more Spanish vessel went down that day. Towards evening, the 605-ton *Maria Juan* of Recalde's squadron signalled desperately to Medina Sidonia that she was sinking. The duke's flagship hurried to the scene, and ordered *Maria Juan*'s crew to abandon ship. But she went down so quickly that only one boatload of her men was rescued: 275 men were lost.

At around 4.00 pm the steadily worsening weather broke in a sudden squall, in which the opposing fleets lost sight of each other. Spanish accounts claimed that Medina Sidonia had wanted to resume the action, but was prevented by the strong winds and currents, which were pushing the Armada in a north-easterly direction. Howard might well have wished to strike the final decisive blow against his shattered opponent, but not only had he once again almost exhausted his

Rations

When available in sufficient quantities, rations for the men of both fleets were reasonably generous.

Spanish

Daily: 1½ lb of biscuit or 2 lb of fresh bread; 1½ pints of wine or 1 pint of stronger Candia wine; 3 pints of water for all purposes.

Sunday and Monday: 6 oz bacon, 2 oz rice.

Monday and Wednesday: 6 oz cheese, 3 oz beans or chick peas

Wednesday, Friday, and Saturday: 6 oz of fish, 3 oz beans or chick peas, 1½ oz of oil, ¼ pint of vinegar.

English

Sunday, Tuesday and Thursday: 1 lb of biscuit, 1 gallon of beer; 2 lb of beef, 4 oz cheese, 2 oz butter

Wednesday Friday and Saturday: 1 lb biscuit, 1 gallon of beer, a quarter of a stockfish or ⅛ of a ling, 4 oz cheese, 2 oz butter.

ammunition, many of his ships were also running out of food and water for their crews. So once again the English fleet pulled back out of range, and resumed their shadowing.

The Battle of Gravelines had been a major English success. This time Howard and his commanders had closed to within effective range, and their heavy guns had wreaked havoc on their opponents. Among the English vessels that had been in the thick of the fighting were Edward Fenton's *Mary Rose*, Robert Crosse's *Hope*, the Earl of Cumberland's *Elizabeth Bonaventure*, the octogenarian Sir George Beeston's *Dreadnought*, Richard Hawkins' *Swallow*, and Sir Robert Southwell's *Elizabeth Jonas*. Notable, perhaps, by his absence, was Sir Francis Drake.

The exact tally of Spanish ships sunk in the day's fighting remains unclear: the English claimed to have accounted for 'five or six great ships'. Spanish accounts mention three, and there was also a report of at least one other, a pinnace, being driven ashore, so the English claim may be approximately correct.

The Spaniards admitted to the loss of 1,000 dead and 800 wounded, who overwhelmed the eighty-five surgeons and their assistants and the two hospital ships. English losses were minimal.

As dusk fell, Medina Sidonia had to face the probability that his enterprise of England was over. But a still greater threat was now looming over the Armada.

Several vivid and detailed accounts of this battle have come down to us, and they deserve to be quoted at length. Medina Sidonia's description to King Philip is the most graphic:

8 August, 6.00 am–Midnight: The Battle of Gravelines

'At dawn on Monday, the 8th, the duke seeing that his Armada was far ahead, and that the enemy was bearing down upon us with all sail, weighed his anchor to go and collect the Armada, and endeavour to bring it back to its previous position. The wind freshened from the NW, which is on to the shore, and the English fleet of 136 sail, with the wind and the tide in its favour, was overhauling us with great speed, whereupon the duke recognised that if he continued to bear room and tried to come up with the Armada all would be lost, as his Flemish pilots told him he was already very near the Dunkirk shoals. In order to save his ships he accordingly determined to face the whole of the enemy's fleet, sending *pataches* to advise the rest of the Armada to luff close, as they were running on to the Dunkirk shoals.

'The enemy's flagship [the *Revenge*], supported by most of his fleet, attacked our flagship with great fury at daybreak, approaching within musket shot and sometimes within arquebus shot. The attack lasted until three in the afternoon, without a moment's cessation of the artillery fire, nor did our flagship stand away until she had extricated the Armada from the sandbanks. The galleon *San Marcos*, with the Marquis de Pimentel on-board, stood by the flagship the whole time. The leading galleass, being unable to follow the Armada, ran aground at the mouth of Calais harbour, followed by some of the enemy's vessels. It is believed that she was succoured by the guns of the fortress of Calais, and that the men on-board of her were saved. Don Alonso de Leiva, Juan Martinez de Recalde, Oquendo's flagship, the whole of the ships of the Castilian and Portuguese Maestros de Campo, Diego Flores' flagship, Bertendona's flagship, the galleon *San Juan* of Diego Flores, with Don Diego Enriquez on-board, withstood the enemy's attack as well as they could, and all of these ships were so much damaged as to be almost unable to offer further resistance, most of them not having a round of shot more to fire.

'Don Francisco de Toledo, who brought up the rear, attempted to close with the enemy. The latter turned upon him with so hot an artillery fire that he was in difficulty. Don Diego de Pimentel then came to his support, but they were both of them being overpowered, when Juan Martinez de Recalde, with Don Agustin Mexia, bore up and extricated them. But notwithstanding this, these two ships once more got into the midst of the enemy, together with Don Alonso de Luzon's ship, the *Santa Maria de Begona*, with Garibay on-board, and the *San Juan de Sicilia*, with Don Diego Tellez Enriquez on-board. They very nearly closed with the enemy without grappling, the English keeping up an artillery fire, from which our men defended themselves with musketry and arquebus fire, as they were so near.

Campaign Chronicle

The duke heard the sound of small arms, but was unable to distinguish what was going on from the maintop, in consequence of the smoke; but he saw that two of our ships were amongst the enemy, and that the latter, leaving our flagship, concentrated all his fleet in that direction, so the duke ordered the flagship to put about to assist them. The duke's ship was so much damaged with cannon shot between wind and water that the inflow could not be stopped, and her rigging was almost cut to shreds, but nevertheless, when the enemy saw that she was approaching, his ships left the vessels they were attacking, namely, those of Don Alonso de Luzon, Garibay, Don Francisco de Toledo, Don Diego de Pimentel, and Don Diego Tellez Enriquez. The three latter were most exposed, and were completely crippled and unserviceable, nearly all the men on-board being either killed or wounded, although that of Don Diego Tellez Enriquez made shift to follow us in very bad case. The duke then collected his force, and the enemy did likewise.

'The duke ordered *pataches* to be sent and take off the men from the *San Felipe*, and the *San Mateo*, but Don Diego Pimental refused to abandon the ship, sending Don Rodrigo Vivero and Don Luis Vanegas to the duke to ask him to send someone on-board to inspect the vessel, and ascertain whether she was seaworthy. The duke sent a pilot and a diver from this galleon, although we were in great risk without him. As the night was falling and the sea was very heavy they were unable to reach the *San Mateo*, but they saw it that night at a distance, falling off towards Zeeland. The galleon *San Felipe* went alongside the hulk *Doncella*, and transhipped on-board of the latter all the company. But when Don Francisco had gone on-board the hulk a cry was raised that she was foundering, and Captain Juan Poza de Santiso leapt on to the *San Felipe* again, followed by Don Francisco. This was a great misfortune, for it was not true that the hulk was sinking, and the *San Felipe* also went towards Zeeland with Don Francisco on-board, after the duke had been informed that he and all his men were safe on the hulk. The sea was so heavy that nothing else could be done, and it was even impossible to patch up the injuries to the flagship; whereby she was in great danger of being lost.

'The duke wished during this day to turn and attack the enemy with the whole armada, in order to avoid running out of the Channel, but the pilots told him it was impossible, as both wind and tide were against us; the wind blowing from the NW towards the land. They said that he would be forced either to run up into the North Sea, or wreck... the Armada on the shoals. He was therefore utterly unable to avoid going out of the Channel, nearly all of our trustworthy ships being so damaged as to be unfit to resist attack,

8 August, 6.00 am–Midnight: The Battle of Gravelines

both on account of the cannon fire to which they had been exposed, and their own lack of projectiles.'

Meanwhile, Pedro de Calderon witnessed the ordeal of the *San Martin*:

'At seven o'clock in the morning the enemy opened a heavy artillery fire on the duke's flagship, which continued for nine hours. So tremendous was the fire that over 200 balls struck the sails and hull on the starboard side, killing and wounding many men, disabling and dismounting three guns, and destroying much rigging. The holes made in the hull between wind and water caused so great a leakage that two divers had as much as they could do to stop them up with tow and lead plates, working all day. The crew were much exhausted by nightfall, with their heavy labours at the guns, without food.

'The *San Felipe* was surrounded by seventeen of the enemy's ships. They directed against her a heavy fire on both sides and on her stern. They approached so close that the muskets and harquebuses of the galleon were brought into service, killing a large number of men on the enemy's ships. They did not dare, however, to come to close quarters, but kept up a hot artillery fire from a distance, disabling the rudder, breaking the foremast, and killing over 200 men in the galleon… [the *San Mateo*, after the engagement] was a thing of pity to see, riddled with shot like a sieve, and had it not been that the duke afterwards sent his divers to her to get the water out of her, she must have gone to the bottom with all hands. All her sails and rigging were torn and sorely destroyed, of her sailors many perished, and of her soldiers few were left.'

Of his own ship, the *San Salvador*, Calderon wrote that she:

'With the duke's flagship engaged an admiral's and a commander's flagship of the enemy, her bows, side, and half her poop being exposed for hours to the enemy's fire, during which time she received no aid. The *San Salvador* had a number of men killed and wounded, and her hull, sails, and rigging so much damaged that she was obliged to change her mainsail. She leaked greatly through the shot holes, and finally the *Rata* [i.e., *Rata Encoronada*] came to her assistance, distinguishing herself greatly. On-board the Rata there fell, killed by a shot, Don Pedro de Mendoza, son of the commander of Castelnuova, Naples, and other persons. The duke's flagship lost forty soldiers; and other persons. The *San Juan de Sicilia*, which carried Don Diego Tellez Enriquez, suffered to such an extent that every one of her sails had

119

The Battle of Gravelines.

to be replaced. Don Pedro Enriquez, who was also on-board, had a hand shot away. The galleon *San Juan* also suffered very severely, as did the *San Marcos*, Don Felipe de Cordoba, son of Don Diego, His Majesty's Master of the Horse, had his head shot off.'

The soldier Pedro Estrada, on-board *San Marcos*, tells of the storm of shot and shell:

'This day was slain Don Felipe de Cordoba, with a bullet which struck off his head and splashed with his brains the greatest friend that he had there, and twenty-four men that were with us trimming our foresail. And where I was with four other men, there came a bullet that struck off the shoe of one of them, without doing any other harm, for they came and plied us very well with shot. And, as I went below in the afternoon, discharging my artillery, there was a mariner that had his leg struck all in pieces and died instantly. The *San Juan de Sicilia*, and the ship of Pedro de Ugerte [the *Maria Juan* of the Biscayan Squadron] and one hulk, remained that day among more than twenty galleons and ships, but they were not boarded but with bullets, and so they delivered themselves and cast about towards us, but very evil entreated.

8 August, 6.00 am–Midnight: The Battle of Gravelines

'Yet the English would not board our ships in any wise, although we did remain and tarryed for them and suffered all their shot of good artillery. And the ship of Pedro de Ugerte remained much spoiled, and we left her, for we had not time to take in all the people. So we bare out of the north and north-east with great disorder, some investing one with another, others separately; and the English in the wind of us discharging their cannons marvellously well, and fired not one piece but it was well employed, by reason we were so nigh one another and they a good space asunder one from the other.'

Richard Tomson, first lieutenant of the *Margaret and John*, described the capture of the *San Lorenzo*:

'It pleased my lord admiral to appoint certain small ships to be fired on Sunday about twelve of the clock at night, and let drive with that flood amongst the Spaniards; which practice, God be thanked, hath since turned to our great good; for it caused the Spaniards to let slip their anchors and cables, and confusedly to drive one upon another; whereby they were not only pit from their roadstead and place where they meant to attend the coming of the Duke of Parma, but did much hurt one to another of themselves; and now by the earnest pursuit of our Englishmen, very much weakened and dispersed, the Lord be praised; so that of the 124 sail that they were in Calais Road, we cannot now find by any account above eighty-six ships and pinnaces; so that I cannot conjecture but by the furious assault that my lord and his associates gave them early on Monday morning, and did continue in vehement manner eight hours, hath laid many of them in the bottom of the sea, or else run with the coast of Flanders to save their lives, though unpossible [*sic*] to save their great ships, by reason of their evil harbours.

'My lord admiral, seeing he could not approach the galleass with his ship, sent off his long boat unto her with but fifty or sixty men, amongst whom were many gentlemen as valiant in courage as gentle in birth, as they well showed. The like did our ship send off her pinnace, with certain musketeers, amongst whom myself went. These two boats came hard under the galleass sides, being aground; where we continued a pretty skirmish with our small shot against theirs, they being ensconced within their ship and very high over us, we in our open pinnaces and far under them, having nothing to shroud and cover us; they being 300 soldiers, besides 450 slaves, and we not, at the instant, 100 persons. Within one half hour it pleased God, by killing the captain with a musket shot, to give us

121

victory above all hope or expectation; for the soldiers leaped overboard by heaps on the other side, and fled with the shore, swimming and wading. Some escaped with being wet; some, and that very many, were drowned. The captain of her was called Don Hugo de Moncada, son to the viceroy of Valencia. He being slain, and the seeing our English boats under her sides and more of ours coming rowing towards her some with ten and some with eight men in them, for all the smallest shipping was nearest the shore, put up two handkerchers upon two rapiers, signifying that they desired truce…'

Sir William Wynter, vice admiral to Lord Henry Seymour, was in the thick of the fighting:

'About nine of the clock in the morning we fetched near unto them, being them thwart of Gravelines. They went into a proportion of a half-moon. Their admiral and vice admiral, went on each side, in the wings, their galleasses, armadas of Portugal, and other good ships, in the whole to the number of sixteen in a wing, which did seem to be of their principal shipping. My fortune was to make choice to charge their starboard wing without shooting of any ordnance until we came within six score [yards] of them, and some of our ships did follow me. The said wing found themselves, as it did appear, to be so charged, as by making of haste to run into the body of their fleet, four of them did entangle themselves one aboard the other. One of them recovered himself, and so shrouded himself among the fleet; the rest, how they were beaten, I will leave to the report of some of the Spaniards that leapt into the seas and are taken up, and are now in the custody of some of our fleet.

'The fight continued from nine of the clock until six of the clock at night, in the which time the Spanish army bare away NNE and N. by E., as much as they could keeping company with one another, I assure your honour in very good order. Great was the spoil and harm that was done unto them, no doubt. I deliver it unto your honour upon the credit of a poor gentleman, that out of my ship there was shot 500 shot of demi-cannon, culverin, and demi-culverin; and when I was furthest off in discharging any of the pieces, I was not out of shot of their arquebus, and most times within speech one of another. And surely every man did well; and, as I have said, no doubt the slaughter and hurt they received was great, as time will discover it; and when every man was weary with labour, and our cartridges spent and munitions wasted – I think in some altogether – we ceased and followed the enemy, he bearing hence still in the course as I have said before.'

8 August, 6.00 am–Midnight: The Battle of Gravelines

Lord Howard's first report to Sir Francis Walsingham was quite brief:

'I have received your letter wherein you desire a proportion of shot and powder to be set down by me and sent unto you; which, by reason of the uncertainty of the service, no man can do; therefore I pray you to send with all speed as much as you can. And because some of our ships are victualled but for a very short time, and my Lord Henry Seymour with his squadron not for one day, in like to pray you to dispatch away our victuals with all possible speed, because we know not whether we shall be driven to pursue the Spanish fleet.

'This morning we drove a galleass ashore before Calais, whither I sent my long boat to board her, where divers of my men were slain, and my lieutenant sore hurt in the taking of her. Ever since we have chased them in fight until this evening late, and distressed them much; but their fleet consisteth of mighty ships and great strength; yet we doubt not, by God's good assistance, to oppress them…

'I will not write to Her Majesty before more be done. Their force is wonderful great and strong; and yet we pluck their feathers by little and little. I pray to God that the forces on land be strong enough to answer so present a force. There is not one Flushinger nor Hollander at the seas. I have taken the chief galleass this day before Calais, with the loss of divers of my men; but Monsieur Gourdan doth detain her, as I hear say. I could not send unto him, because I was in fight; therefore I pray you to write unto him, either to deliver her, or at leastwise to promise upon his honour that he will not yield her up again to the enemy.'

Later, writing more leisurely in his 'official' despatch, Howard was able to give more details:

'By reason of [the fireship attack] the chief galleass came foul of another ship's cable and brake her rudder, by means whereof he was forced the next day to row ashore near the haven's mouth and town of Calais; whereupon the lord admiral sent his long boat, under the charge of Amyas Preston, gentleman, his lieutenant, and with him Mr Thomas Gerrard and Mr Harvey together with other gentlemen, his lordship's followers and servants, who took her and had the spoil of her. There entered into her about 100 Englishmen. And for that she was aground, and could not be gotten off, they left her to Monsr. Gourdan, Captain of Calais, where she lieth sunk.

'Now that the Lord Henry Seymour and Sir William Wynter were joined with us, our fleet was near about 140 sail – of ships, barks and pinnaces etc., the lord admiral, Sir Francis Drake in the *Revenge*, accompanied with Mr Thomas Fenner in the *Nonpareil* and the rest of his squadron, set upon the fleet of Spain and gave them a sharp fight. And within short time, Sir John Hawkins in the *Victory*, accompanied with Mr Edward Fenton in *Mary Rose*, Sir George Beeston in the *Dreadnought*, Mr Richard Hawkins in the *Swallow*, and the rest of the ships appointed to his squadron, bare with the midst of the Spanish army, and there continued hotly; and then came the lord admiral, the Lord Thomas Howard, the Lord Sheffield, near the place where the *Victory* had been before, where these noblemen did very valiantly.

'Astern of these was a great galleon assailed by the Earl of Cumberland and Mr George Raymond in the *Bonaventure* most worthily, and being also beaten with the Lord Henry Seymour in the *Rainbow*, and Sir William Wynter in the *Vanguard*, yet she recovered into the fleet. Notwithstanding, that night, she departed from the army and was sunk. After this, Mr Edward Fenton in the *Mary Rose* and a galleon encountered each other, the one standing to eastward and the other to westward, so close as they could conveniently pass by one another, wherein the captain and company did very well. Sir Robert Southwell that day did worthily behave himself, as he had done many times before; so did Mr Robert Crosse in the *Hope*, and most of the rest of the captains and gentlemen. This day did the Lord Henry Seymour and Sir William Wynter so batter two of the greatest armadoes that they were constrained to seek the coast of Flanders, and were afterwards, being distressed and spoiled, taken by the Zeelanders and carried into Flushing. In this fight it is known that there came to their end sundry of the Spanish ships, besides many other unknown to us.'

Sir Francis Drake, in customary brisk style, gave Walsingham a short account of the battle:

'This bearer came aboard the ship I was in in a wonderful good time, and brought with him as good knowledge as we could wish. His carefulness therein is worthy [of] recompense, for that God hath given us so good a day in forcing the enemy so far to leeward as I hope in God the Prince of Parma, and the Duke of Sidonia shall not shake hands this few days; and whensoever they shall meet, I believe neither of them will greatly rejoice this day's service. The town of Calais hath seen some part thereof, whose Mayor Her Majesty is beholden unto. Business commands me to end. God bless Her Majesty, our gracious sovereign, and give us all grace to live in his fear. I assure your honour this day's service hath much appalled the enemy, and no doubt but encouraged our army.'

Robert Cecil, one of the commissioners pursuing abortive negotiations with Parma, spoke to a Spanish eyewitness:

'I thought it good to acquaint you with that which I heard of a Spanish gentleman taken yesterday in one of the galleasses, which was run ashore at Calais, and there is seized by Monsr. Gourdan. The captain of this ship, named Moncada, one of the greatest personages in the fleet, was killed with a small shot of musket that pierced both his eyes. The second of account in that ship is taken and kept in one of the ships in Her Majesty's fleet. This man that is here is a proper gentleman of Salamanca, who affirmeth that there is great lack imputed to the Duke of Parma, in that he hath not joined with this fleet which hath lingered about Calais and Gravelines of purpose for him, and would not have stirred from those roads, if the device of the fireworks on Sunday had not forced them to slip their anchors and so make head away, in which instant my lord admiral gave them that fight which we saw upon the land yesterday; where, terrible as it was in appearance, there was few men hurt with any shot, nor any one vessel sunk. For, as this man reporteth, they shoot very far off; and for boarding, our men have not any reason.'

A French fisherman, however, saw something of the true nature of the battle:

'He saw some ships broken into bits, others without masts or sails, from which they were throwing overboard artillery, trunks and many other things, whilst men were striving to save themselves by escaping in boats, with such lamentation as may be imagined.'

The Battle of Gravelines would prove to have been the decisive engagement of the Armada Campaign. Unfortunately, the confused nature of most contemporary accounts leave some frustrating gaps in our knowledge of the exact course of events. Certainly, however, it was not as great a victory for the English as has often been claimed. There were only four certain Spanish losses, though one or more smaller vessels may also have gone down, as Howard and his commanders believed. There could be no certainty the Armada might not offer battle again, in which case few of the English commanders were confident of the outcome.

Yet in many ways the seven or eight hours of intense fighting that day had been a traumatic experience for the Spaniards, and would prove to have destroyed any will among the majority to renew the fight. This was not so much because of the losses suffered as a result of close-range English gunnery, but the final realisation that the English could never be brought to fight on Spanish terms. It was clear that, except through some unlikely turn of events, the Spaniards would not be able to grapple and board any of their elusive opponents, while their own gunnery techniques were hopelessly ineffective in comparison with English practice.

In terms of their conduct of the battle, Medina Sidonia is deserving of rather more praise than Howard. The duke had fought a courageous rearguard action that had given the Armada time to reform its shattered formation, and without which the transport ships might well have been hunted down like sheep. And, although some of his commanders may have shirked the fight, the hard core of veterans like Oquendo, Recalde, and de Leiva, had stood by their commander against everything the English could hurl against them.

The picture on the English side was less impressive. Howard's decision to detach his entire squadron for two hours in a partially successful attempt to deal with the *San Lorenzo*, undoubtedly weakened the English attack on the main body of the Armada during the critical period when it was still disorganised and vulnerable. Drake's actions are also obscure, although lack of information makes it impossible to estimate how well he played his part. The main credit for English success that day lies with the squadron led by Lord Henry Seymour and Sir William Wynter. Fresher than the rest of the fleet, and going into action with their ammunition as yet undepleted – though possibly only amounting to about twenty shot per gun – it was they who seem to have inflicted most of the damage on the enemy.

But no matter how incomplete it was tactically, strategically, the Battle of Gravelines was a major English success. Not only was any juncture between Parma and Medina Sidonia now highly unlikely, the Armada had been pushed out of the Channel and into the North Sea, where it risked yet greater danger.

Tuesday 9 August: 'The Most Fearful Day in the World'
Wind and Weather: strong NW wind until dawn then alternating changes to SW then strong SSW; sea rough

While the fighting at sea had been raging, English preparations to meet what seemed to be an imminent landing by Parma's veterans were continuing.

Efforts to muster troops had continued with mixed success, many militia units disbanding themselves once the apparent threat to their own localities had passed: so the plan for shadowing the Armada's progress up-Channel with a growing militia force marching along the coast never really took off.

The Earl of Leicester – since 24 July acting as 'lieutenant general of the

9 August: 'The Most Fearful Day in the World'

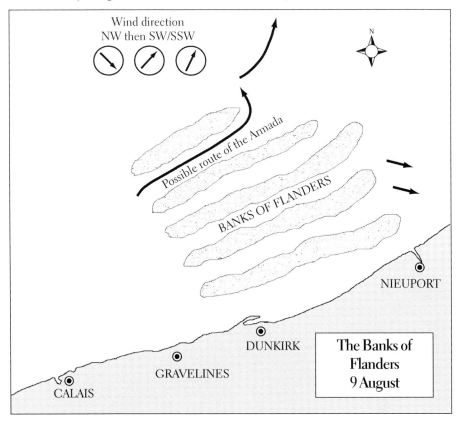

queen's armies and companies' – remained convinced the main threat was to the east of England. By early August, he apparently mustered some 5,000 foot and a few hundred horse at Tilbury camp for the defence of London. How far Leicester – not a perceptive man and in any case suffering from exhaustion and ill-health – fully appreciated the weakness of his situation is unclear. As we have seen, the Kentish militia were ill-prepared to meet a major landing. Leicester's levies, on the whole, were not a great deal better, while their camp at Tilbury was not only on the wrong side of the Thames, but as the elaborate pontoon bridge (designed by the Italian engineer Gambelli) was as yet incomplete, there was no quick way for Leicester's forces to cross the river in the event of a Spanish landing in Kent.

As Drake's old antagonist, Sir William Burroughs, discovered when commissioned to inspect the defences of the Thames, preparations were woefully inadequate. The great defensive chain that Gambelli had erected across the lower reaches of the river had been swept away by the first spring tide, while fortifications defending the approaches to London were few and half-built. Burroughs himself was given command of one rather unseaworthy galley, with which to bar the river against the might of the Armada. He accurately surmised that the best use to which it could be put was to be sunk as a block ship in the middle of the river in the case of any Spanish attack.

Elizabeth had wanted to appoint Leicester, her long-time favourite and perhaps one-time lover, as Lieutenant General of all England and Ireland, but this had been opposed by the queen's other councillors, who argued such a move would be politically unwise, making the ambitious Leicester very close to being treated as heir to the throne. They had also wanted to move Elizabeth away from London even before any invasion began, but the queen was determined to remain in full control of the defensive preparations.

Knowing the queen's character perhaps better than anyone, Leicester wrote to her on 6 August, suggesting she might care to visit the camp at Tilbury: 'You shall comfort not only these thousands, but many more that shall hear of it.' Elizabeth was delighted, and her visit duly took place on 18 August.

It was a superb piece of Elizabethan theatre, in which the fading middle-aged spinster, with red wig and rather incongruous back and breast plates, was transformed, at any rate in the assurances of her admirers, into a warrior queen, who rode with her officers amidst the massed ranks of her troops, and perhaps, delivered to some of them something like the inspiring speech credited to her in a broadsheet published a few days later.

None of this, of course, would have made a successful resistance to Parma's landing any more likely. But though none of those at Tilbury that day yet knew it, the danger was virtually over.

Parma's troops had actually begun embarking on their invasion barges on 9 August when they heard the sound of heavy and continuous firing from out at sea. Next morning, with news of the reverse off Gravelines coming in, Parma disembarked his men and marched them back to camp. He knew, possibly with a good deal of relief, that barring a totally unlikely change of fortune, any prospect of the Army of Flanders having to make an invasion attempt was at an end.

At sea, dawn found the Armada in its greatest peril so far. All night, the Spaniards had been only too aware that the north-westerly winds were carrying them inexorably closer to the dreaded Banks of Flanders: 'Hardly a man slept that night. We went along, all wondering when we should strike one of the banks.' As morale collapsed, an unknown number of the Armada's men requisitioned ships' boats and rowed desperately for the shore in an attempt to escape.

All night the English fleet shadowed their seemingly doomed opponents. At some stage during the hours of darkness the captain of a stricken vessel of Diego Flores De Valdez' squadron, possibly *La Trinidad*, attempted to surrender, but the ship went down with all hands before terms could be agreed.

9 August: 'The Most Fearful Day in the World'

In the dawn light the Spaniards could see the Banks looming ever nearer as the depth of water beneath their keels dwindled, and the English drifted implacably just out of cannon range, content to allow nature to complete the destruction of the enemy.

Aboard some of the Spanish ships discipline broke down in the face of imminent death. Even Medina Sidonia's flagship was not immune, as quarrels broke out among the duke's staff. One of them, Luis de Miranda, remembered: 'we saw ourselves lost or taken by the enemy, or the whole armada drowned upon the banks. It was the most fearful day in the world, for the whole company had lost all hope of success and looked only for death.'

The duke was urged either to surrender or to take the Holy Banner and board a pinnace to seek safety ashore but coolly refused. As Oquendo's ship passed close by, Medina called to him – apparently somewhat desperately – for advice. The bitterness of this veteran seaman towards the duke's unpopular chief of staff erupted as Oquendo replied curtly: 'Ask Diego Flores. As for me, I am going to fight and die like a man.'

Calling together his pilots, who included one renegade Englishman and a Fleming – probably the only ones who knew these waters well – Medina Sidonia asked them whether it might be possible to reach a German or Norwegian port in order to refit, or even now seize an English or Dutch port as refuge. The pilots were understandably doubtful, and pointed out that unless the wind changed, the entire Armada was likely to be lost.

By about 10.00 am, the *San Martin*'s leadsmen were reporting only six fathoms of water beneath her keel. The duke fired signal guns in an attempt to rally the Armada, whose vessels had apparently again lost formation. But with the banks on one flank and the enemy on the other, it seemed there could be no escape.

The Banks of Flanders were, in fact, rather more complex in formation than some accounts suggest. The degree of danger they presented depended partly on the state of the tide. At high tide they were roughly 6 fathoms below the surface, a depth which was just about sufficient for most of the Armada to clear. But at low water they were a mere 3 fathoms below the surface, and in some places only 2 fathoms or less: clearly fatal for Spanish vessels unfortunate enough to strike there. To add to the complications facing Medina Sidonia and his pilots, most of the banks were long and narrow, with channels of deeper water lying between them, where the Spanish ships might be safe, if they managed to cross the banks flanking them. The problem was that nobody knew exactly where these channels were, or the exact position of the Armada in relation to them.

For some time, the *San Martin* seems to have sailed with one of her remaining anchors down, in the hope that it might gain a grip on the sea bottom before the flagship struck.

Campaign Chronicle

The wind now seemed to be rising, and the sea growing rougher, and the Spaniards were still unable to gain any searoom. Medina Sidonia had with him the redoubtable hard core of his fighting ships, including Recalde's *San Juan*, de Leiva's *Rata Encoronada*, *San Marcos*, a Castilian galleon, and the three surviving galleasses. Whatever the rest of the Armada did, the commanders of these seven ships were ready to die with their captain general.

The seas breaking on the Banks of Flanders were now clearly visible, but then, whether by an act of God – as claimed by the Spaniards – or more prosaically, a normal meteorological event at that time of day in those waters, the wind swung to its more usual south-south-westerly direction. Slowly, the Armada pulled clear of danger and back on to a northerly course.

Howard and his commanders made little comment on the Armada's escape, which they may have regarded as the result of a commonplace, if disappointing, trick of the weather. Lack of ammunition made it unwise to engage the enemy again, especially as, so long as the wind continued to carry the Spaniards further and further into the North Sea, there was no pressing need to do so. For the present, Howard was content to continue shadowing the Armada.

That afternoon, with the danger of being driven ashore fast receding, Medina Sidonia called a council of war aboard the *San Martin*. Full details of what was probably a fairly fraught meeting have not survived, but the outlines of what happened are clear. Medina Sidonia summarised the current state of the Armada, and its shortage of 'great shot', then, his choice of words clearly indicating his own views, the duke asked the council 'whether it would be best to return to the Channel, or sail home to Spain by the North Sea, the Duke of Parma not having sent advice that he would be able to come out promptly.'

Despite this clear hint, not all of the council agreed with the duke. Both Diego Flores and Recalde favoured returning to the Channel, and eventually their opinion, theoretically at least, carried the day, when the council decided unanimously in favour of returning to the Channel if the weather would allow it, and of sailing back to Spain via the North Sea if it did not.

It is clear that these words were designed to placate King Philip. Nobody had any real intention or expectation of returning to the English Channel. Apart from anything else, the south-south-westerly wind – now rising towards gale force – was driving the Armada ever more rapidly further into the North Sea. What is also clear is that Medina Sidonia, having performed, on the whole, very capably in the earlier stages of the campaign, was by now both exhausted and despairing. Neither he, nor, so far as the records reveal, any of his commanders had suggested the alternative of seizing a port on the east coast of England.

In a further indication of something approaching mental and physical collapse, Medina Sidonia now retired to his cabin, handing over direction of the Armada to the military commander Bobadilla, probably assisted by de Leiva and the sick Recalde. The duke had been angered by the debacle of the previous day, when a number of his captains had ignored orders to rally around the flagship. Bobadilla now sent a pinnace round the fleet with the warning that any commander who allowed his ship to get ahead of the flagship would be court martialled and executed.

Howard held his own council of war. It was clear that, except in case of dire necessity, the shortage of ammunition would prevent the English fleet from engaging the Spaniards again. There was also still a lingering fear that Parma might take advantage of the absence of the English fleet to slip across the Channel. To guard against this, a protesting Lord Henry Seymour – reluctant to quit a possible scene of action – was ordered to leave the fleet under cover of darkness and resume his old station in the Straits of Dover. Howard and the remainder of the fleet would continue to track the Armada northwards as far as the Firth of Forth, after which it would no longer pose an immediate threat to English territory.

Medina Sidonia reported to King Philip the day's events:

'Tuesday the 9th, eve of St Lorenzo. At two o'clock in the morning the wind blew so strongly that although our flagship was brought up as close to the wind as possible, she began to fall off to leeward towards the Zeeland coast, the duke's intention having been to stay so that he might again enter the Channel.

'At daybreak the NW wind fell somewhat, and we discovered the enemy's fleet of 109 ships rather over half a league astern of us. Our flagship remained in the rear with Juan Martinez de Recalde, Don Alonso de Leiva, the galleasses, and the galleon *San Marcos* and *San Juan* of Diego Flores: the rest of the Armada being distant and a great deal to leeward. The enemy's ships bore down on our flagship, which came round to the wind and lay to; the galleasses placed themselves in front, and the rest of our rearguard stood by ready to repel the attack, whereupon the enemy retired. The duke then fired two guns to collect the Armada and sent a pilot in a *patache* to order the ships to keep their heads close to the wind, and they were almost on the Zeeland shoals. This prevented the enemy from approaching closer to us, as they saw that our armada was going to be lost; indeed the experienced pilots who accompanied the duke assured him at this time that it was impossible to save a single ship of the Armada, as they must inevitably be driven by the north-west wind on to the banks of Zeeland. God alone could rescue them. From this desperate peril, in only

6½ fathoms of water, we were saved by the wind shifting by God's mercy to the SW, and the Armada was then able to steer a northerly course without danger to any of our ships.

'The orders sent by the duke in the *pataches* were that the whole of the ships were to follow in the wake of the flagship, otherwise they would run upon the banks. The same afternoon the duke summoned the generals and Don Alonso de Leiva to decide what should be done. The duke submitted the state of the Armada, and the lack of shot, a fresh supply of which had been requested by all the principal ships; and asked the opinion of those present as to whether it would be best to return to the English Channel, or sail home to Spain by the North Sea, the Duke of Parma not having sent advice that he would be able to come out promptly. The council unanimously resolved in favour of returning to the Channel if the weather would allow of it, but if not, then that they should obey the wind and sail to Spain by the North Sea, bearing in mind that the Armada was lacking all things necessary, and that the ships that had hitherto resisted were badly crippled. The wind from the SSW kept increasing in violence, and the duke continued to get further out to sea, followed by the whole of the enemy's fleet.'

Captain Alonso Vanegas of the *San Martin* describes the desperate hours when the Armada seemed doomed to destruction:

'The duke was advised that if he wanted to escape with his life he would have to surrender. It was impossible to avoid being driven aground. He replied that he trusted in the favour of God and His Blessed Mother to bring him to a port of safety; he would not question the faith of his ancestors. People appealed to his conscience not to allow so many souls to be lost by shipwreck, but he would not listen to such advice and told them to speak no more of the matter. He summoned the pilots, among whom were an Englishman and a Fleming, the rest being Spanish, Basque or Portuguese. He discussed with them whether it would be possible to reach Hamburg or the Norwegian coast, or to attack some other harbour to save part of the fleet. They all replied that they would make every effort, but were doubtful of success unless God helped them with a miracle, and shifted the wind so that they could get out to open sea. The duke ordered three shots to be fired to summon our fleet to rejoin him. Soundings were taken again, and the flagship was found to be now in 6 fathoms. It could be seen that the wind was blowing her down on the Zeeland shoals, which stick out 3 leagues into the sea. But on the other flank was the enemy fleet.

9 August: 'The Most Fearful Day in the World'

It seemed to everyone that we could neither save the ships nor reform the fleet to renew the attack on the enemy. We were expecting to perish at any moment. The duke was not convinced by these opinions, which showed such lack of courage, and Don Francisco de Bobadilla was of one mind with him in saying everyone must trust that God would deliver them.'

Richard Tomson felt that the Armada was now virtually beaten:

'At this instant, we are as far to the eastward as the Isle of Walcheren, wherein Flushing doth stand, and about 12 leagues off the shore; and the wind hanging westerly, we drive our enemies apace to the eastward, much marvelling, if the wind continues, in what port they will direct themselves. There is want of powder, shot and victual amongst us, which causeth that we cannot so daily assail them as we would, but I trust Her Majesty, may, by God's help, little fear any invasion by these ships, their power being, by battle, mortality, and other accidents, so decayed, and those that are left alive so weak and hurtless, and they could be well content to lose all charges to be at home, both rich and poor.'

Though no English commander voiced the thought in his correspondence, 9 August must have been an intensely frustrating day for Howard and his men. All morning the Armada seemed on the verge of destruction by being wrecked on the Banks of Flanders, only to be saved by a last-minute change in wind direction. Even more frustrating was their inability to complete the battering they had inflicted on the Spaniards on the previous day, due to lack of ammunition. It was obviously not politic for the official English account of the campaign to mention the constant problems that shortages of supplies – of all kinds – had caused the English fleet: but that there was widespread anger and frustration among Elizabeth's seamen is obvious from a comment from Henry Whyte to Sir Francis Walsingham that 'our parsimony at home hath bereaved us of the famousest victory that ever our navy might have had at sea.'

Despite the successes off Gravelines, Howard knew that if the wind changed, the Spaniards might turn and fight, and he could do little more than put on a brave front and shadow them, hoping that his bluff would not be called.

There were those among the Spanish leadership, notably Recalde, who would have dearly liked to do just that, but they were clearly in a minority. Medina Sidonia had had enough, and most of his men would have agreed with him. If the promised ammunition from Parma had arrived in time, the council of war's decision might have been different, but it must be questioned whether the morale of their men had not crumbled too far to make another battle possible. The

Armada's policy of leaving crippled ships to their fate – first demonstrated off Plymouth and reinforced after the action at Gravelines – had struck a major blow at both officers' and men's confidence in their senior commanders. And their morale was about to slump still further.

10–12 August: The End of the Threat

Wind and Weather: wind generally SSW and strong; seas heavy

Throughout 10 August the strong south-south-westerly wind hurried the Spaniards on northwards, with the English fleet remaining on their heels, just out of gunshot range. At one point, the Armada again shortened sail, as if to offer battle, an invitation which Howard declined. But even as Medina Sidonia, or Bobadilla, who seems to have been in effective command, made their challenge, there was further apparent evidence of falling morale as at least two Spanish ships ignored orders and continued on northwards. It would later be claimed in a secret report for Philip II compiled by Don Juan de Cordona that 'after they left the Channel the majority thought of nothing but to steer their course and get back to Spain.'

Although Howard may have been heartened by evidence of Spanish indiscipline, he had his own problems. Many of the commanders of the smaller privately owned ships in his fleet felt they had done their duty once the Spaniards had been harried out of the Channel, and had begun slipping away home. As well as ammunition shortages, supplies of all kinds were running desperately short in the remainder of the fleet, and after another council of war, the English commanders sent their decision to the queen, signed by all of them as a measure of self-protection against royal wrath: 'we whose names are hereunder written have determined and agreed in council to follow and pursue the Spanish fleet until we have cleared our own coast and brought the Firth [of Forth] west of us; and then to return back again, as well to revictual our ships, which stand in extreme scarcity, as also to guard and defend our coast at home: with further protestation that, if our wants of victuals and munition were supplied, we would pursue them to the furthest that they durst have gone.'

Next day, 11 August, Bobadilla took his revenge for the lapses in discipline that had dogged the Armada. No less than twenty captains were arraigned or summarily condemned for 'having behaved badly and for being cowardly'. Some, it appears, were accused of offences relating to the action off Gravelines, but at least two were condemned for failing to obey orders on 10 August. All were apparently condemned to death by a summary court martial, presided over by Bobadilla. One, Don Cristobal de Avila, of the hulk *Santa Bárbara*, was paraded through the fleet then hung at the masthead of a pinnace. A second officer, Captain Francisco de Cuellar of the Castilian galleon, *San Pedro*, was also condemned for sailing ahead of the flagship on 10 August, though Cuellar claimed it had been done while he was asleep, by a 'wicked pilot' in order to repair damage suffered off Gravelines. After being condemned by Bobadilla, Cuellar was fortunate enough to be sent for sentencing to the ship of the judge advocate of the Armada, a friend who allowed him to send word of his plight to Medina Sidonia. The latter was apparently still in the state of despondency, which had gripped him ever since the Battle of Gravelines, and as Cuellar wrote: 'kept his cabin and was very unhappy and did not want anybody to speak to him.' The duke – apparently ignorant of what had been ordered in his name – reprieved Cuellar: but not Don Cristobal.

Next morning, the opposing fleets arrived off the Firth of Forth. Howard half-expected the Spaniards to attempt to enter the Forth: possibly to assist Scottish Catholic malcontents rise against the government of James VI. He was prepared to fight in order to prevent this, but contingency plans proved unnecessary, as the Armada continued on its northern course. It was time for the English fleet to turn back for home, leaving a pinnace and a caravel to shadow the Spaniards until they were beyond Orkney and the Shetland Isles.

Though nobody could yet be certain of it, the last shots of the Armada Campaign had been fired, but for many of the men on both sides, the ordeal was just beginning.

Medina Sidonia was both brief and evasive when he reported the events of the day to the king:

'On Friday, the 12th, at dawn, the enemy's fleet was quite close to us, but as they saw we were well together, and that the rearguard had been reinforced, the enemy fell astern and sailed towards England until we lost sight of him. Since then we have continued sailing with the same wind until we left the Norwegian Channel, and it has been impossible for us to return to the English Channel even if we desired to do so.'

Thomas Fenner accurately prophesied the fate of the Armada:

'I verily believe great extremity shall force them if they see England again. By all that I can gather they are weakened of eight of their best sorts of shipping, which contained many men; also many wasted in sickness and slaughter. Their masts and sails much spoiled; their pinnaces and boats many cast off and wasted; wherein they shall find great wants when they come to land and water, which they must shortly do or die; and where or how, my knowledge cannot imagine. As the wind serveth, no place but between the Foreland and Hull. If the wind by change suffer them, I verily believe they will pass about Scotland and Ireland to draw themselves home; wherein, the season of the year considered, with the long course they have to run and their sundry distresses, and – of necessity – the spending of time by watering, winter will so come on as it will be to their great ruin…'

Aftermath

—◦•⟨◦⟩•◦—

When on 12 August, Medina Sidonia decided that the Armada should return to Corunna via the North Sea, looping around the Shetlands into the Atlantic, and then, avoiding the poorly charted and treacherous coast of Ireland, steer south through the Atlantic for home, he was following a sound course of action, which would have been supported by any experienced seaman. At this stage, although the Armada had had the worst of its encounter with the English fleet, and had failed in its objective of covering an invasion of England by the Army of Flanders, it had not suffered a decisive defeat. It still seemed entirely possible that the fleet could return to Corunna, spend the winter re-fitting, and then, with its losses replaced, renew the contest if King Philip so ordained.

The duke's immediate concerns were the battle damage suffered by many of his ships, and his supplies of food and water. He had set out from Corunna with about two months' supplies, so should have had just over half remaining. As a precaution, in order to conserve water, Medina Sidonia ordered all the horses and mules with the Armada to be thrown overboard, and then resumed his voyage.

From the beginning, the Spaniards found the weather a more formidable foe than Howard or Drake had been. Struggling against contrary north-westerly winds, sometimes veering to the south-west, the Armada did not enter the Atlantic until 20 August. Almost immediately the Spaniards encountered worsening weather, as rising gales scattered many of the hulks and previously damaged ships far to the north and east. A trickle of losses began and inexorably increased.

One Spaniard later recalled that: 'from the 24th to the 4th of September we sailed without knowing whither, through constant storms.' The damage sustained by the hulls of many ships, particularly in the Gravelines action, meant the stormy seas opened their seams, making ships still less seaworthy, and causing some (mainly hulks at this stage), to founder. Other vessels, having proceeded a considerable way south towards their destination, not only failed to make further progress, but were actually driven back almost as far as they had come, into the North Atlantic.

137

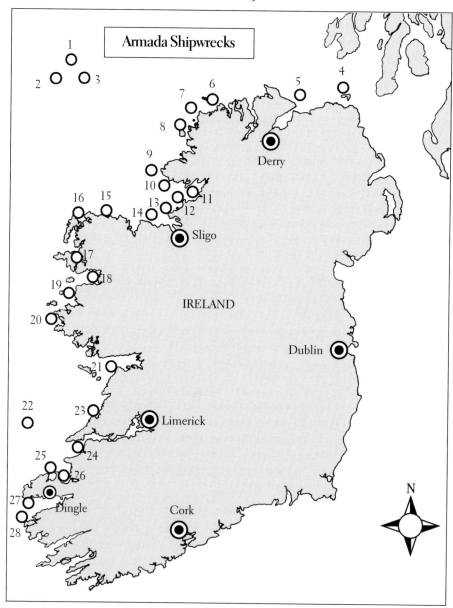

Armada Shipwrecks

Derry

Sligo

IRELAND

Dublin

Limerick

Dingle

Cork

N

By 3 September, presumably with further problems from spoiled and unusable water and supplies, Medina Sidonia was noting anxiously: 'I pray God in his mercy will grant us fine weather so that the Armada may soon enter port; for we are so short of provisions that if for our sins we are long delayed, all will be irretrievably lost. There are now a great number of sick and many die.'

By the middle of September, with the Armada now caught in the tail end of a

Aftermath

Key to Map of Armada Shipwrecks

1	*Castillo Negro*	15	*La Rata Encoronada*
2	*Barcade Amberg*	16	*Unknown*
3	*Santiago*	17	*El Gran Grin*
4	*Girona*	18	*Falcon Blanco Mediano*
5	*Trinidad*	19	*Unknown*
6	*Unknown*	20	*Unknown bulk*
7	*Unknown*	21	*San Esteban*
8	*Duquesne Santa Ana*	22	*Anunciada*
9	*Unknown*	23	*Unknown*
10	*Unknown*	24	*Unknown*
11	*Juliana*	25	*Santa Maria de la Rosa*
12	*Lavia*	26	*Unknown*
13	*Santa Maria de Vison*	27	*San Juan Batista*
14	*Unknown*	28	*Unknown*

hurricane, which had come much further east than usual, Medina Sidonia's ships were scattered across hundreds of miles of ocean from western Ireland almost as far north as Ireland. Desperately short of supplies – especially water – and with their vessels battered almost to destruction by the savage seas, a number of ships, including a group led by Recalde, who had some knowledge of these waters, headed for the Irish coast. During the next fortnight, ship after ship foundered or met its end on the rocky coastline of western Ireland. Those who managed to reach shore were often robbed, sometimes slaughtered, but more usually assisted by the native Irish population. But the English authorities in Ireland, fearful of an uprising supported or incited by the Spanish survivors, adopted a policy of killing virtually all they were able to round up.

Perhaps the most notable of several thousand Spaniards who, from mid-September through to about the end of October, met their end either in the seas off Ireland, on its rocks, or at the hands of man, was Alonso de Leiva: drowned in the wreck of the galleass *Girona*. All told, at least twenty-three ships of the Armada we lost on the Irish coast, including such stalwarts of the Channel battle as *La Rata Encoronada*, *Duquesna Santa Ana*, and *Girona*.

It was these losses on the voyage home that turned a reverse into a major Spanish disaster.

It was early September when the first rumours of a setback for the Armada began to reach Spain. King Philip's first reaction was puzzled disbelief: 'I hope that God has not permitted so much evil,' he scribbled on one report, 'for everything has been done for His service.'

Medina Sidonia's own messenger, carrying news of the failure of the expedition – though not of the disaster which subsequently ensued – reached Philip on 24 September. Three days earlier, Medina Sidonia himself, with eight ships, had limped into Corunna, while other survivors reached ports dotted along the coast of northern Spain. The duke reported to the king that 'the misfortunes and miseries that have befallen us... are the worst that have been known on any voyage.' Stricken with illness, Medina Sidonia struggled to organise assistance for his thousands of sick, starving, and dying crewmen. Among the notables who died soon after reaching harbour were the already sick Juan Martinez de Recalde, and Miguel de Oquendo: the latter probably from the effects of a wound suffered in the fighting.

By mid-October it was becoming obvious that few, if any, of the remaining missing ships of the Armada would ever be seen again. Philip admitted the full extent of the catastrophe, commenting after studying a report of the disaster in Ireland: 'I have read it all, although I would rather not have done, because it hurts so much.'

It was now apparent that perhaps as many as seventy vessels of the Armada had failed to return. Some of the hulks and smaller ships may have reached port without being recorded, but at the lowest estimate perhaps one-third of the fleet's 130 ships had been lost: and others, including some of its finest fighting ships, were so badly damaged either not to be worth repairing or likely to be out of action for many months.

In contrast to the attitude of Elizabeth and her ministers, King Philip did not neglect or unduly blame the survivors of his armada. Medina Sidonia – who, rather regrettably, only waited for his arrears of pay before departing – was allowed to return home, and was never blamed by the king: though others were less charitable. It was felt, however, that a scapegoat was needed, and the choice fell on Diego Flores de Valdez – though he got off quite lightly with an eighteen-month prison sentence. As for the humble rank and file of the Armada, Philip endeavoured to ensure the sick and wounded were cared for, and that all received their arrears of pay prior to discharge.

The treatment of Howard's victorious seamen was far different. For some time after the Armada disappeared into the northern mists, there was uncertainty in England regarding the enemy's future intentions, and ignorance regarding his fate. Howard and his commanders warned that Medina Sidonia might refit in some Scandinavian port and return to join Parma, who, likened by Drake to 'a bear robbed of his whelps', might yet attempt an invasion on his own account.

Indeed, whether to cover himself with the king, or in case the Armada indeed returned, the Army of Flanders was not stood down, nor its invasion flotilla dispersed, until the end of August.

Consequences

Queen Elizabeth, notoriously parsimonious, had ordered the troops at Tilbury to begin disbanding on 20 August, and her attention turned next to her fleet.

Although not a single ship of the English fleet had suffered serious damage in the fighting, and battle casualties had been extremely light, even before Howard's ships began to return to port, sickness was sweeping through his crews. In the *Elizabeth Bonaventure*, for example, 200 of the 500 men with whom she had sailed from Plymouth in July were dead a month later. Howard warned that a similar rate of loss among the 16,000 men crowded in unsanitary conditions aboard his ships was virtually inevitable. In September, he wrote desperately to the privy council that: 'it would grieve any man's heart to see them that have served so valiantly die so miserably.' But Lord Burghley, echoing the views of Queen Elizabeth, responded coldly that: 'by death, by discharging of sick men, and such like, there may be spared something in the general pay.'

Howard was horrified, protesting that: 'It were too pitiful to have men starve after such a service' and trying to appeal to the government's self-interest by pointing out: 'if men should not be cared for better than to let them starve and die miserably, we should hardly get men to serve.'

His words failed, however, to move the queen and her ministers, and in the end the only relief offered to the crews was that provided by the efforts of their own commanders. Howard was particularly generous in supplying some of the more urgent needs out of his own pocket. In 1590 he, Drake, and Hawkins, set up a fund for 'poor sailors maimed in the navy' – later known as the 'Chatham Chest' – by which small deductions were taken from sailors' pay (assuming they ever received it) to sustain a pension and compensation fund for seamen

This, however, came too late for many of the men of the fleet of 1588. How many died through sickness and neglect cannot be known for sure: but perhaps up to half were dead by winter – roughly the same rate of loss as in the Armada.

Consequences

The defeat of the Armada neither ended the war nor broke the power of Spain. Though one Spanish writer described the reverse as 'the greatest disaster to strike Spain in 600 years,' Philip's empire was strong and resilient enough to survive the blow. Within weeks the king had come to the conclusion that victory over Elizabeth had 'become all the more necessary because of what has happened'.

Energetic efforts began to strengthen the armed forces, and more particularly, to rebuild and reorganise the navy. Among its fruits were the construction of a dozen galleons: the famous 'Twelve Apostles', designed and armed on English lines, while Martin de Bertendona, the most experienced surviving squadron commander of the Armada, was to advise on the best way of making another assault on England.

The 'Other' Armadas

P hillip II's immediate reaction, on learning that his Armada had failed, was to declare that the war would go on. During the following years, several further major naval expeditions were mounted against England.

Delayed by English counterstrokes and the need to rebuild his fleet, Philip's second Armada did not sail until October 1596. Commanded by Don Pedro de Zubiaur, a force of 126 vessels – half of them warships – sailed to strike at the West Country or Ireland. The Queen's Ships were mostly in port, refitting, and only a sudden storm on 18 October, which caught the Spaniards off the Galician coast – sinking over thirty ships and forcing the rest back to port – saved Elizabeth from almost certain disaster.

In 1597, while the bulk of the English fleet, under the Earl of Essex, was operating ineffectively off the Azores, Philip tried again. On 9 October, Don Martin de Padilla, with 136 ships carrying 9,000 troops, sailed in an attempt to seize the Cornish port of Falmouth as a bridgehead and trap Essex's fleet on its return home.

Once again, the elements saved England. The Spaniards were within 30 miles of Falmouth when, on 18 October, another savage storm shattered Padilla's fleet, sinking twenty-eight ships and driving the rest back to port.

The Spanish government, now under King Philip III, remained undeterred, although the cost of the war was increasingly draining her resources. In 1599 there were rumours in England of yet another armada sailing from Corunna. But in the event, this 'Invisible Armada', as it was termed, sailed south against Dutch raiders.

It was not until 1601, in the dying years of the war, that a Spanish armada at last made landfall, when 3,000 Spanish troops were disembarked at Kinsale in south-west Ireland, in support of the faltering rebellion of the Earl of Tyrone. But they had come too late: English forces defeated Tyrone and forced the surrender of his Spanish allies.

Philip would despatch two more armadas against England: one in 1596 and another the following year. Both were driven back by storms. After Philip's death in 1598, his son and successor, Philip III, would despatch yet another abortive expedition, and rather more successfully – initially, at least – sent troops to aid the Earl of Tyrone's rebels in Ireland.

Elizabeth, likewise – though her actions were still limited by financial considerations – was eager to follow up the defeat inflicted on Medina Sidonia. In 1589, a joint Anglo-Dutch expedition, financed largely by private speculators, was despatched under Drake to strike at the northern Spanish ports and finish off the remnants of the Armada. It proved to be an almost unqualified failure. Although three Spanish vessels, including Recalde's old flagship *San Juan*, and Bertendona's *Regazona*, were destroyed in an attack on Corunna, Drake then allowed himself to be diverted into a futile attempt to capture Lisbon, thus triggering a Portuguese uprising. With its inevitable failure, the expedition – having also bungled an attempt to intercept the annual treasure *flota* – stumbled home. Drake was in disgrace for several years to come.

England would launch other major expeditions, with some successes – notably the brief capture of Cadiz in 1596 – but her main exploits were carried out by the privateers, who, year after year, took a steady toll of Spanish trade and shipping in a constant harrying, which aided by the Dutch, spread right across Philip's worldwide empire.

On land, English forces continued to aid the Dutch rebels, and in France, provided assistance to the new Protestant king, King Henry IV, who was engaged in a civil war against Catholic rebels, allied with Spain.

By 1604, with both Elizabeth and Philip dead, Henry victorious in France, the Irish rebellion crushed, and the conflict in the Netherlands deadlocked, both England and Spain were ready to end an increasingly costly war, and agree to a peace that basically recognised the current status quo.

Judgement of History

Though it would take several more decades before the decline of Spain became an apparent and acknowledged fact, the defeat of the Armada would be seen with hindsight as being the beginning of that process. It is worth considering, therefore, whether its failure was inevitable, and indeed how close it came to success.

The problem that dogged Spanish efforts from the early stages of planning was the decision to make the 'Enterprise of England' a joint operation per-formed by the Army of Flanders and a fleet from Spain. Coordination would always have been difficult, and communication delays between Medina Sidonia and Parma made matters worse. King Philip must also share a major portion of the blame because of his failure to clarify the confusion over exactly where the rendezvous between Parma and the Armada was to take place – even after the differences in views between his two commanders had become clearly apparent.

Don Francisco de Bobadilla, as a participant, summed up the problem while tactfully avoiding pointing the finger of blame at any of the major participants: 'I don't know who had the idea that we could join forces in a place with such powerful currents, with a shore so open and liable to cross-winds, and with so many sandbanks… But I believe that it is impossible to control all the things that must be concerted at the same time, in order to bring together forces that are so separated, unless one has a different sort of ship from those we brought, in the place where we were instructed to join.'

In fact, Bobadilla was not entirely correct in his summary. A major factor was that Medina Sidonia and Parma had not been ordered to rendezvous off Calais. The Armada had anchored there because it had received no news of Parma, and could not sail any further without effectively abandoning any hope of joining him.

Contemporaries tended to put the blame for this situation on Parma, suggesting he had never had any intention of attempting to carry out the invasion of England, and may even have been contemplating a deal with Elizabeth, which would have established him as ruler of an independent Netherlands. Parma was aware of these and similar suggestions, and strongly protested his innocence, at the same time blaming Medina Sidonia for the campaign's failure.

So far as Parma is concerned, while he probably became increasingly dubious about the prospects of success for the projected invasion, there is nothing to suggest he did not carry out the necessary preparations with competence and thoroughness: if not with alacrity. Once he learned of the Armada's arrival off Calais, he began embarking his troops according to plan, and most of them, according to the inspector-general of the Armada, an eyewitness, were aboard their transports when the Armada disappeared into the North Sea, following the action off Gravelines.

So if Parma fulfilled his part, was Medina Sidonia to blame?

Too much emphasis has been placed upon the duke's protestations of unsuitability at the time of his appointment. As we have seen, he had all the qualities regarded as necessary in a captain-general, and throughout the campaign appears to have readily listened to, and accepted, advice from the experienced naval commanders around him. He provided courageous and determined leadership in action, on more than occasion helping retrieve a dangerous situation.

The main difficulties facing Medina Sidonia were the failure to maintain adequate communications with Parma, and the nature of his orders from the king. The former was the result of a mixture of circumstances and bad luck, which should, however, have been anticipated in the overall planning of the operations. The latter failing was almost entirely the fault of the king.

During the operations in the Channel, Medina Sidonia was constantly hamstrung by his orders from Philip to avoid fighting a major action with the English fleet, if at all possible. It quickly became apparent to the Armada's commanders that only by fighting, and winning, such an action, would the way be open for Parma to join them in the open sea. Although the duke naturally did not admit as much in his report to the king, the Spaniards on more than one occasion attempted to bring on a decisive engagement with the enemy, only to be frustrated by Howard's refusal to comply.

There has been much debate regarding the effectiveness, or otherwise, of the tactics employed by the opposing fleets. The notion that the Spaniards wanted only to close and board with their opponents – and were surprised by the English refusal to allow this to happen – is an over-simplification. An engagement of this nature was clearly what the Spaniards, with their large numbers of troops, hoped for: but they were also prepared to fight a fairly long-range artillery duel. In this, Medina Sidonia had but little success, due to the unwillingness of the English to close to effective range. The net result was that the duke wasted a good deal of his scarce ammunition. In the rather ineffectual probing and skirmishing, which characterised most of the early fighting in the Channel, the Spanish deficiencies in gun-handling were less apparent, and partly cancelled out by the failure of the English gunners to inflict any serious damage. The two Spanish ships lost during this stage of the campaign were victims of circumstance, not of enemy action.

By the time he anchored in Calais Roads. Medina Sidonia had, in fact, successfully carried out the first stage of the orders given him by the king. The problems he then faced were the result of the failings in those orders, and the inability to coordinate his movements with those of Parma. Even so, the margin of failure was very narrow. If Medina Sidonia's messengers had reached Parma slightly earlier, and the Army of Flanders had been able to begin embarking only twenty-four hours sooner, there would have been every chance of the two forces attempting to unite. Whether, in the face of a united and undefeated English fleet, they would have had any prospect of being able to attempt a landing in England is much more doubtful.

The result of the Battle of Gravelines, when the opposing fleets at last came to close quarters, suggests that the 'Enterprise of England' would have been doomed in any case. However, we should perhaps be cautious in assuming such a result was inevitable. At Gravelines, the Armada was attacked while suffering from serious disadvantages. And even then, Medina Sidonia was able to pull his fleet together and at a heavy – though not crippling cost – manage to hold off the English attack until such time as Howard ran out of ammunition. If the Armada had entered the battle prepared and in effective fighting formation, it is by no means certain that Medina Sidonia could not have thwarted the English fleet long enough for Parma to have made his landing in Kent. And if this had occurred, English prospects would have been bleak.

As Bobadilla – no particular friend of Medina Sidonia – concluded: 'Even his enemies will admit, although it may grieve them, that no commander in the world has done more than this one.'

So it is equally unfair to blame either Medina Sidonia or Parma for a failure that should more appropriately be laid at the door of King Philip. The latter's unwillingness to recognise and address the failings of a plan that became apparent even before the Armada had left Spanish waters, or to take proper account of the misgivings of his commanders, was the main reason for what happened. When faced with the clear evidence of the impracticability of his scheme, Philip's assumption that the Almighty would provide the necessary miracle to bring about victory, was a clear abdication of responsibility and a refusal to face reality.

Writing a few years later, Sir Walter Ralegh concluded: 'To invade by sea upon a perilous coast, being neither in possession of any port, nor succoured by any party, may better fit a prince presuming on his fortune than enriched with understanding.'

Given the difficulties which the Spaniards faced, how far was the failure of the Armada due to the efforts of its English opponents?

Howard and his commanders faced another obstacle almost as threatening as the enemy. Queen Elizabeth and some of her privy council, by their equivocation and reluctance to commit money and resources, frequently frustrated attempts to devise and sustain a coherent strategy against the threat of the Armada. It was largely because of the late arrival of essential supplies that, in July, Howard and his fleet, while in the Bay of Biscay, were almost thrown off-balance by the departure of the Armada from Corunna, and failed to reach the port before Medina Sidonia sailed.

For virtually the entire campaign, Howard was dogged by ammunition shortages, which seriously reduced his ability to inflict damage on the enemy. This was not, however, the only reason for the English lack of success. During the series of engagements in the Channel, contemporary critics noted an apparent unwillingness of English commanders to come close enough to the Spaniards to do them serious harm. This was sometimes put down to 'coldness' or timidity. The more probable reasons were that Howard was still experimenting with unfamiliar tactics, and also that English command and control was frequently ineffective – much more so than was the case with the hard core of the Armada's fighting ships. Drake, who did not particularly distinguish himself during the campaign, was a prime example of this, when he went off on his totally unauthorised foray to capture the *Rosario*, and imperilled the rest of the fleet in the process. In justice to Drake, it must be said that Howard himself behaved in similar impulsive and irresponsible fashion off Calais, when he took his entire squadron to attack the crippled galleass *San Lorenzo*, taking his ships out of the main action for several critical hours, and disrupting the agreed plan of attack on the Armada.

Judgement of History

It is difficult to escape the conclusion that the English were extraordinarily lucky. The fireship attack on the Armada in Calais Roads was made by too few ships, inadequately prepared, against an enemy who was on the alert and had made preparations for just such an eventuality. The odds were stacked heavily on its failing, and it was a remarkable stroke of good fortune for Howard when the attack succeeded. Without it, it is unlikely the English fleet could have broken the Spanish formation and prevented them linking up with Parma in the following twenty-four hours.

Only at Gravelines did the English fleet at last come close enough to the enemy for their superior and more effective gunnery to begin having significant effect. But even then they were unable to prevent the Armada from regaining its formation, and Howard was forced to call off his attack in late afternoon, partly because of worsening weather, but primarily because of his recurrent shortage of ammunition.

Fortunately, the Spaniards had had enough, and as a result of the fireship attack, the failure to make contact with Parma, and the battering they had suffered at Gravelines, their already fragile morale finally broke. It remains something of a mystery why Medina Sidonia did not consider the option of re-fitting in a Scandinavian port more seriously. The most likely explanation is that his spirit, and those of most of his men, had been broken. The events of the previous week had convinced them that the 'Enterprise of England' faced an impossible task.

Finally, to borrow the words of a later British commander, the Armada Campaign had been a very 'close-run thing' indeed.

Biographical Notes

Spanish

Alonso de Bazan, Marquis of Santa Cruz (1526–88). The original organiser and intended commander of the Armada. An experienced naval commander who led the Neapolitan galley squadron in 1568, and played an important role in the Battle of Lepanto (1571). He commanded the Spanish naval forces in the Azores (1582–83), and in 1584 was appointed 'captain-general of the ocean sea' (effectively commander in chief of the Spanish fleet).

Martin de Bertendona. Commander of the Levant Squadron of the Armada. A member of a leading Spanish seafaring family. Bertendona's father had commanded the ship that took King Philip to England for his marriage to Queen Mary.

Francisco de Bobadilla. Commander of the army units aboard the Armada, and military adviser to Medina Sidonia.

Alonso de Leiva (1540–88). A former captain-general of the galleys of Naples and later captain-general of Milanese cavalry. A favourite of Philip II, de Leiva had campaigned in North Africa, and in 1576, against the Dutch. He took part in the conquest of Portugal in 1580.

Juan Gomez de Medina (d.1588). An experienced seaman, Medina was transferred from the command of a galleon to lead the Squadron of Hulks with the Armada. He was lost with his flagship off Ireland.

Alonso Perez de Guzman ('El Bueno'), Duke of Medina Sidonia (1550–1619). Head of one of the wealthiest and most influential families in Spain, Medina Sidonia was a well-regarded administrator. As Captain of Andalusia, he had been responsible for overseeing preparations made at Cadiz for the Armada. Although his previous experience of active military command was limited, Medina Sidonia displayed considerable personal courage during the Armada Campaign, and given the difficulties of the task set him, and the limitations of the king's orders, proved rather more competent than is often acknowledged.

Diego de Medrano. Commander of the Portuguese galley squadron, which was forced to leave the Armada during rough weather in the Bay of Biscay.

Hugo de Moncada (d.1588). An expert in galley warfare, Moncada led the Neapolitan galleass squadron of the Armada.

Augustin de Ojeda. Commander of the *patache* squadron of the Armada.

Miguel de Oquendo (d.1588). Commander of the Squadron of Guipuzcoa. Oquendo was a courageous fighter, whose exploits during the Azores Campaign (1582–83) had earned him the nickname of 'the Glory of the Fleet'.

Alessandro Farnese, Duke of Parma (1545–92). A nephew of King Phillip, Parma fought in the great naval victory over the Turks at Lepanto (1571), and had already proved himself to be a capable soldier when he was made governor of the Netherlands. A skilful organiser as well as fighting commander, Parma reorganised and revitalised the Army of Flanders, and by a mixture of military ability, diplomacy, and occasional ruthlessness, gradually reconquered much of the Netherlands from the Dutch rebels. His outstanding achievement was probably the capture of Antwerp in 1585. An ambitious man, Parma was never entirely trusted by King Philip.

Philip II (1527–98). Ruler of an empire that extended throughout most of the known world. As he grew older, Philip became firmly set in his beliefs: convinced of his divinely-appointed role in defeating the enemies of Catholicism. Leading a life of relative simplicity in his monastic-like quarters at the Escorial Palace, Philip became increasingly reluctant to delegate, and his attempt to micro-manage the Armada Campaign was a principal cause of its failure.

Juan Martinez de Recalde (1526-88). A native of Bilbao, northern Spain, Recalde served the Spanish Crown for over twenty years. He was closely involved in shipping operations on the route between the Netherlands and Spain. Between 1572 and 1580 Recalde commanded Spanish naval forces operating in the Netherlands, and in 1580 he commanded the ships that took troops to Smerwick in Ireland. In 1582–83 he commanded a squadron in the Azores Campaign.

Biographical Notes

Recalde was one of Spain's most experienced seamen.

Diego Flores de Valdez. A seasoned mariner with long experience of the Atlantic and West Indies trade routes, as well as being a noted map-maker and ship designer. Nominally commander of the Castilian Squadron of the Armada, Diego Flores served as Medina Sidonia's chief of staff aboard the flagship *San Martin.* He was unpopular with his fellow commanders, mainly because of his bad temper.

Pedro de Valdez. A veteran of the Azores Campaign, de Valdez commanded the Squadron of Andalusia. Cousin of Diego Flores de Valdez, the two men were, for unknown reasons, bitter enemies.

Anglo-Dutch

William Cecil, Lord Burghley (1520–98). Elizabeth's lord high treasurer and chief minister from 1578, Burghley dominated the political scene in England. He was closely involved with English planning for the Armada Campaign.

Sir Francis Drake (?1542–96). Son of a Devon 'hedge-preacher', Drake was partially motivated in his bitter feud with Spain by his Protestant beliefs, but arguably even more so by hopes of booty. An outstanding seaman and charismatic leader, Drake was intolerant of any opposition. During his Circum-navigation of the Globe, he had one critic, Thomas Doughty, executed on a dubious charge of treason. Drake, who became a wealthy man on the proceeds of his privateering expeditions, was not a 'team player', and on several occasions proved unable to subordinate his privateering instincts to the wider objective.

Elizabeth I (1533–1603). Daughter of Henry VIII and Anne Boleyn, Elizabeth's right to the throne was rejected by most of Catholic Europe, which held her to be illegitimate. Highly intelligent, but capricious and with a tendency to procrastinate, Elizabeth feared the consequences and expense of war with Spain, and followed a dangerous and ambiguous course by tacitly encouraging the activities of privateers such as Drake, while officially denying any involvement. She had little of the religious commitment of many of her contemporaries, and was mainly concerned with preserving the balance of power in Europe in order to safeguard English interests.

Thomas Fenner (d.1590). Drake's flag captain in the Indies expedition of 1585, and probably vice admiral in the Cadiz raid of 1587.

Armada 1588

Sir Martin Frobisher (c.1537–94). A Yorkshireman, Frobisher was involved in the slave trade between Africa and Spanish America. During the 1560s he was a privateer, and possibly a pirate. In the following decade he made three voyages of exploration in search of the North West Passage between the Atlantic and the Pacific. Frobisher was a tough argumentative man, but a notable fighter.

Sir John Hawkins (1532–95). A 'rough, masterful man', Hawkins was at various times a merchant, slave trader, and privateer. In 1578 he was appointed treasurer of the navy. As well as improving general efficiency, Hawkins also encouraged developments in ship design, notably the evolution of the 'race-built' galleon. A skilful tactician, Hawkins lacked Drake's impulsiveness.

Robert Dudley, Earl of Leicester (?1532–88). Elizabeth's favourite, and possibly her lover. In 1585 he was placed in command of the English forces sent to the Netherlands, but angered the queen in the following year by his assumption of the title of 'governor general of the Netherlands'. He was reconciled with the queen on his return to England in 1588, and despite an uninspiring military performance in the Netherlands, Leicester was given command of the main field army mustered at Tilbury. He fell sick and died a few weeks after the campaign was over.

Justin of Nassau (1559–1631). An illegitimate son of William I of Orange, Justin served under his father in the fighting in Zeeland, and in 1588 was appointed lieutenant admiral of Zeeland, with the task of blockading the Spanish-held ports in Flanders.

Sir John Norris (?1547–97). Known as 'Black Jack', Norris was a professional soldier who had fought for many years in Ireland, France, and the Low Countries. In 1588 he was marshal of the camp at Tilbury, as well as organising defence preparations across much of southern England. He was disliked by the Earl of Leicester, who was jealous of Norris's experience and military reputation.

Charles Howard, Lord Effingham, later Earl of Nottingham (1531–1624). Howard was a cousin of Queen Elizabeth. Following in the footsteps of his great grandfather, father and two uncles, Howard was appointed lord admiral of England in 1585. He had no previous experience of naval command, but proved forceful and far-sighted in lobbying government over the needs of the navy. He was probably better as a naval administrator than in the task of leading and coordinating a fleet in battle.

Biographical Notes

Lord Henry Seymour (b.1540). An experienced seaman appointed 'admiral of the narrow seas' in 1588. His task was to protect English shipping in the eastern English Channel and guard against raids or landing attempts by the Spanish forces in Flanders.

Sir Francis Walsingham (1530–90). A puritan in religion and a leading supporter of the war against Spain. Walsingham began his career as an intelligence gatherer for Lord Burghley. In 1573 he became a secretary of state and organiser of the queen's intelligence apparatus.

Sir William Wynter (d. 1589). Lord Seymour's vice admiral, Wynter (sometimes referred to as 'Winter' in contemporary sources) was one of England's most experienced seaman. He had fought with success against the French early in Elizabeth's reign, and had commanded a Queen's Ship in the Smerwick Campaign of 1580. As 'surveyor of the Navy', he was involved with Hawkins in the rebuilding of the English fleet after 1578.

Orders of Battle

———— ⊷ ⫸(●)⫷ ⊶ ————

Army of Flanders

On paper, the Spanish Army of Flanders – commanded by Alexandre Farnese, Duke of Parma – totalled 59,915 men in April 1588. But after necessary deductions had been made for internal security and the continuing conflict with the Dutch rebels, the numbers available for the invasion of England were significantly smaller, though not apparently as few as the 17,000 sometimes claimed.

In July 1588 the units earmarked for the invasion included:

Don Sancho de Leiva's Tercio, quartered at Verne, Winox, Bergues, and Diksmuide

Don Juan Marique de Lara's Tercio at Ypres,

Don Francisco de Bobadilla's Tercio at Bailluel

The Catalan Tercio at Warneton.

When it was learnt that the Armada was at Calais, these and other troops were all moved to Dunkirk to begin embarking.

In theory a full-strength Spanish or Italian *tercio* had twelve companies, averaging 250 men plus eleven officers, with a total strength of 2,190 pikemen, 448 arquebusiers and 230 musketeers. German, Burgundian, and Walloon troops had a slightly different organisation, and were formed into regiments, each of ten companies of thirty men, with pikemen and 'shot' in equal proportions. Cavalry units, which included lancers and mounted arquebusiers, were organised in 100-strong companies.

The total invasion force (with some units still under-strength despite recruiting efforts) seems to have consisted of:

Spaniards: 6,000 men (four *tercios*)

Italians: 3,000 men (two *tercios*)

Irish: 1,000 men (mainly defectors from the English forces in Holland under the renegades Rowland Yorke and William Stanley)

Burgundians: 1,000 men (one regiment)

Walloons: 7,000 men (seven regiments)

Germans: 8,000 men (four regiments)

Cavalry: 1,000 men (twenty-two companies)

Total: 27,000 men

The Armada

(under 'Fate', '+' indicates a vessel that survived the campaign, 'X' indicates a loss, '?' indicates fate unknown, '—' indicates data unknown)

Squadron of Portugal

Name of Ship	Tons	Guns	Soldiers	Mariners	Total Men	Commander	Fate
San Martin (fleet flagship)	1,000	48	300	177	477	Capt. Marolin De Juan+	
San Juan de Portugal (vice admiral's ship)	1,050	50	321	179	500		+
San Marcos	790	33	292	117	409	Marquis de Penefiel	X Ireland
San Felipe	800	40	415	117	532	Juan de Santiso	X off Flanders
San Luis	830	38	376	116	492	Don Augustin Mexia	+
San Mateo	750	34	277	120	397	Don Diego Pimentel	X off Flanders
Santiago	520	24	300	93	393		+
Florencia	961	52	400	86	486	Gaspar de Sosa	+ (but unfit for further service)
San Cristobel	352	20	300	78	378		+
San Bernardo	352	21	250	81	331		+
Augusta (zabra)	166	13	55	57	112		+
Julia (zabra)	166	14	44	72	116		+

Totals:

12 ships, 7,737 tons, 387 guns, 3,330 soldiers, 1,293 mariners, 4,623 total crews, 9 ships survived

Name of Ship	Tons	Guns	Soldiers	Mariners	Total Men	Commander	Fate
Squadron of Castile							
San Cristóbal (flagship)	700	36	205	120	325		+
San Juan Bautista (vice admiral's ship)	750	24	207	136	343	Marcos Aramburu	+
San Pedro	530	24	141	131	272	Francisco de Cuellar	+?
San Juan	530	24	163	113	276	Don Diego Enriquez	X Ireland
Santiago el Mayor	530	24	210	132	342		+
San Felipe y Santiago	530	24	151	116	267		+
La Asunción	530	24	199	114	313		+
Nuestra Señora del Barrio	530	24	155	108	263		+
San Medel y Celedon	530	24	160	101	261		+
Santa Ana	250	24	91	80	171		+
Nuestra Señora de Begoña	750	24	174	123	297		+
La Trinidad	872	24	180	122	302		X Ireland?
La Santa Catalina	882	24	190	159	349		+
San Juan Bautista	650	24	192	93	285	Gregoria Melandez	X Ireland
Nuestra Señora del Socorro (patache)	75	24	20	25	45		X (possibly stayed at Flanders)
Antonio de Padua (patache)	75	12	20	46	66		X (possibly stayed at Flanders)

Totals:
16 ships, 8,714 tons, 384 guns, 2,458 soldiers, 1,719 mariners, 4,147 total crews, *c.* 13 ships survived

Name of Ship	Tons	Guns	Soldiers	Mariners	Total Men	Commander	Fate
Biscayan Squadron							
Santa Ana	768	30	256	73	329	Nicolas de Isla	X
El Gran Grin (vice admiral's ship)	1,160	28	256	73	329	A. Felipe	X Ireland
Santiago	666	25	214	102	316		+
La Concepción de Zubelzu	486	16	90	70	160		+
La Concepción de Juanes del Cano	418	18	164	61	225	Juan del Cano	X Ireland
La Magdalena	530	18	193	67	260		+
San Juan	350	21	114	80	194		+
La María Juan	665	24	172	100	272	Pedro de Ugarte	X Gravelines
La Manuela	520	12	125	54	179		+
Santa María de Monte-Mayor	707	18	206	45	251		+
La María de Aguirre (patache)	70	6	20	23	43		?
La Isabella (patache)	71	10	20	22	42		+
Patache de Miguel Suso (patache)	36	6	20	26	46		?
San Estaban (patache)	96	6	20	26	46		+

Totals:

14 ships, 6,543 tons, 238 guns, 1,870 soldiers, 822 mariners, 2,692 total crews, c. 10 ships survived

Name of Ship	Tons	Guns	Soldiers	Mariners	Total Men	Commander	Fate
Andalusian Squadron (Don Pedro De Valdez)							
Nuestra Señora Del Rosario (flagship)	1,150	46	304	118	422		X surrendered
San Francisco (vice admiral's ship)	915	21	222	56	278		+
San Juan	810	31	245	89	334		+
San Juan de Gagarin	569	16	165	56	221		+
La Concepción	862	20	185	71	256		+
Duquesna Santa Ana	900	23	280	77	357	Don Alonso De Leiva	X Ireland
Santa Catalina	730	23	231	77	308		+
La Trinidad	650	13	192	74	266		+
Santa Maria del Juncal	730	20	228	80	308		+
San Bartolomé	976	27	240	72	312		+
El Espirtu Santo (patache)	33	10	—	—	43		?

Totals:
11 ships, 8,292 tons, 240 guns, 2,325 soldiers, 780 mariners, 3,105 total crews, c. 9 ships survived

Name of Ship	Tons	Guns	Soldiers	Mariners	Total Men	Commander	Fate
Guipuzcoan Squadron (Don Miguel de Oquendo)							
Santa Ana (flagship)	1,200	47	303	82	385		X blew up at San Sebastian
Nuestra Señora de la Rosa	945	26	233	64	297	Martin de Villafrance	X Ireland
San Salvador	958	25	321	75	396		X surrendered

Name of Ship	Tons	Guns	Soldiers	Mariners	Total Men	Commander	Fate
San Esteban	736	26	196	68	264		X Ireland
Santa Marta	548	20	173	63	236		+
Santa Barbara	525	12	154	45	199		+
San Buenaventura	379	21	168	53	221		+
La Maria San Juan	291	12	110	30	140		+
Santa Cruz	680	16	156	32	188		+
Doncella (urca)	500	16	156	32	188		X Santander
La Asuncion (patache)	60	9	20	23	43		?
San Bernabé (patache)	60	9	20	23	43		+
Nuestra Señora de Gaudalupe	1	15	—	—	—		?
Magdalena	1	14	—	—	—	?	

Totals:
15 ships, 6,691 tons, 241 guns, 2,010 soldiers, 619 mariners, 2,600 total crews, c. 9 ships survived

Levantine Squadron (Don Martin de Bertendona)

Name of Ship	Tons	Guns	Soldiers	Mariners	Total Men	Commander	Fate
La Regazona (flagship)	1,249	30	344	80	424		+
La Lavia (vice admiral's ship)	728	25	203	71	274		X Ireland
La Rata Encoronada	820	35	335	84	419		X Ireland
San Juan de Sicilia	800	26	279	63	342	Don DiegoTellez Enriquez	X Scotland
La Trinidad Valencera	1,100	42	281	79	360	Don Alonso de Luzon	X Ireland
La Anunciada	703	24	196	79	275	Capt. O. Iveglia	X Ireland

Name of Ship	Tons	Guns	Soldiers	Mariners	Total Men	Commander	Fate
San Nicholas Prodaneli	834	26	374	81	455	Capt. Maria Prodaneli	X Ireland
La Juliana	860	32	325	70	39,5	Don F. de Aranada	X Donegal
Santa Maria de La Vison	666	18	236	71	307	Capt. J. de Bartolo	X Ireland
La Trinidad de Scala	900	22	307	79	386		+

Totals:

10 ships, 8,754 tons, 280 guns, 2,880 soldiers, 757 mariners, 3,637 total crews, 2 ships survived

Squadron of Hulks or Urcas (Don Juan Gomez de Medina)

Name of Ship	Tons	Guns	Soldiers	Mariners	Total Men	Commander	Fate
El Gran Grifón (flagship)	650	38	243	43	286		X Ireland
San Salvador (vice admiral's ship)	650	24	218	43	261	Pedro Coco De Calderon	+
Perro Marina	200	7	70	24	94		+
Falcon Blanco Mayor	500	16	161	36	197		+
Castillo Negro	750	27	239	34	273	Capt. Pedro Ferrat	X Ireland
Barca de Amberg	600	23	239	25	264	Capt. Juan de San Martin	X Ireland
Casa de Paz Grande	650	26	198	27	225		+
San Pedro Mayor (hospital ship)	581	29	213	28	241		X Devon
El Sanson	500	18	200	31	231		+
San Pedro Menor	500	18	157	23	180		?
Barca de Anzique	450	26	200	25	225	Capt. Pedro de Arechaga	?
Falcón Blanco Mediano	300	16	76	27	103	Don Luis de Cordoba	X Ireland

Name of Ship	Tons	Guns	Soldiers	Mariners	Total Men	Commander	Fate
Santo Andres	400	14	150	28	178		+
Casa de Paz Chica	350	15	162	24	186		+
Ciervo Vólante	400	18	200	22	222	Capt. Juan de Permato	X Ireland
Paloma Blanca	250	12	56	20	76		+
La Ventura	160	4	58	14	72		+
Santa Barbara	370	10	70	22	92		?
Santiago	600	19	56	30	86	Capt. J.H. de Luna	X Ireland
David (Chico)	450	7	50	24	74		?
El Gato	400	9	40	22	62		+
Esayas	260	4	30	16	46		+
San Gabriel	280	4	35	20	55		?

Totals:
23 ships, 10,251 tons, 384 guns, 3,121 soldiers, 608 mariners, 3,729 total crews, c. 16 ships survived

Pataches and Zabras (Don Antonio Hurtado de Mendoza)

Name of Ship	Tons	Guns	Soldiers	Mariners	Total Men	Commander	Fate
Nuestra Señora de Pilar de Zaragosa (flagship)	300	11	109	51	160		?
La Caridad	180	12	70	36	106		?
San Andrés	150	12	40	29	69		?
El Crucifijo	150	8	40	29	69		?
Nuestra Senora Del Puerto	55	8	30	33	66		?

Name of Ship	Tons	Guns	Soldiers	Mariners	Total Men	Commander	Fate
La Concepción De Carasa	70	5	30	42	72		?
Nuestra Señora de Regona	64	20	26	46			?
La Concepción de Capetillo	60	10	20	26	46		?
San Jeronimo	50	4	20	37	57		?
Nuestra Señora de Gracia	57	5	20	34	54		+
La Concepción de Francisco de Latero	75	6	20, 29	49			?
Nuestra Señora de Guadalupe	70	—	20	42	62		+
San Francisco	70	—	20	37	57		?
Esperitu Santo	75	—	20	47	67		+
Trinidad (zabra)	—	2	—	23	23		X Ireland
Nuestra Señora de Castro	—	2	—	26	26		?
Santo Andres	—	—	—	15	15		?
La Concepción de Valmaseda	—	—	—	27	27		?
La Concepción	—	—	—	31	31		?
Santa Catalina	—	—	—	23	23		?
San Juan de Carasa	—	—	—	23	23		?
Asuncion	—	—	—	23	23		?

Totals:

22 ships, 1,426 tons, — guns, — soldiers, — mariners, 1,168 total crews, ? ships survived

Name of Ship	Tons	Guns	Soldiers	Mariners	Total Men	Commander	Fate
Galleasses of Naples (Don Hugo de Moncada)							
San Lorenzo (flagship)	50	262	124	386			X Calais
Zúñiga	50	178	112	290			+
Girona	50	169	120	289		Capt. Fabrico Spinola	X Ireland
Napolitana	50	264	112	376			+

Totals:

4 ships, — tons, 200 guns, 728 soldiers, 368 mariners, 1,096 total crews, 2 ships survived

Portuguese Galleys (Don Diego Medrano)							
Capitana (flagship)	—	5	56	53	109		+
Princesa	—	5	37	44	81		+
Diana	—	5	32	47	79		X Bayonne
Bazana	—	5	26	46	72		+

Totals:

4 ships, — tons, 20 guns, 151 soldiers, 190 mariners, 341 total crews, 3 ships survived

Orders of Battle

The English Fleet

Name of Ship	Commander	Tons	Guns	Crew
Plymouth Fleet (Lord Charles Howard)				
Queen's Ships (14)				
Ark Royal	Lord Charles Howard	800	38	430
Elizabeth	Earl of Cumberland	600	34	250
Golden Lion	Lord Thomas Howard	500	34	250
White Bear	Lord Sheffield	1,000	66	490
Elizabeth Jonas	Sir Robert Southwell	900	54	490
Victory	Sir John Hawkins	800	44	450
Triumph	Martin Frobisher	1,100	46	500
Dreadnought	Sir George Beeston	400	26	190
Mary Rose	Edward Fenton	600	36	250
Swallow	Richard Hawkins	360	26	160
Foresight	Christopher Baker	300	26	150
Scout	Henry Ashley	100	16	70
George Hoy	Richard Hodges	100	—	20
Armed Merchant Vessels (33)				
Hercules of London	George Barne	300	—	120
Toby of London	Robert Barrett	250	—	100
Galleon	Dudley James Erisay	250	—	96
Centurion of London	Samuel Foxcraft	250	—	100
Minion of Bristol	John Sachfield	230	—	110
Mayflower of London	Edward Bancks	200	—	90
Ascension of London	John Bacon	200	—	100
Primrose of London	Robert Bringborne	200	—	90
Margaret & John of London	John Fisher	200	—	90
Tiger of London	William Caesar	200	—	90
Red Lion of London	Jervis Wilde	200	—	90
Minion of London	John Dale	200	—	90
Edward of Maldon	William Pierce	186	—	30
Gift of God of London	Thomas Luntlowe	180	—	80
Bark Potts	Anthony Potts	180	—	60
Bark Burr of London	John Serocold	160	—	70
Brave of London	William Furthow	160	—	70
Royal Defence of London	John Chester	160	—	80
Nightingale	John Doate	160	—	16
John Trelawney	Thomas Meek	150	—	30

Armada 1588

Name of Ship	Commander	Tons	Guns	Crew
Cure's Ship	—	150	—	—
Golden Lion of London	Robert Wilcox	140	—	70
Thomas Bonaventure of London	William Aldridge	140	—	70
Samuel of London	John Vassall	140	—	50
White Lion	Charles Howard	140	—	50
Crescent of Dartmouth	—	140	—	75
Bartholomew of Topsham	Nicholas Wright	130	—	70
Unicorn of Bristol	James Langton	130	—	66
Angel of Southampton	—	120	—	—
Robin of Sandwich	—	110	—	—
Galleon of Weymouth	Richard Miller	100	—	—
John of Barnstaple	—	100	—	65
Charity of Plymouth	—	100	—	—

Additions: 89 vessels under 100 tons

Western Squadron (Sir Francis Drake)
Queen's Ships (5)

Name of Ship	Commander	Tons	Guns	Crew
Revenge	Sir Francis Drake	500	36	250
Nonpareil	Thomas Fenner	500	34	240
Hope	Robert Crosse	600	33	280
Swiftsure	Edward Fenner	400	28	180
Aid	William Fenner	250	23	120

Armed Merchant Vessels (21)

Name of Ship	Commander	Tons	Guns	Crew
Galleon Leicester	George Fenner	400	—	160
Merchant Royal	Robert Ficke	400	—	140
Roebuck	Jacob Whiddon	300	—	120
Edward Bonaventure	James Lancaster	300	—	120
Gold Noble	Adam Seagar	250	—	110
Galleon Dudley	James Erisay	250	—	96
Hopewell	John Merchant	200	—	100
Griffin	William Hawkins	200	—	100
Minion of London	William Winter	200	—	80
Thomas Drake	Henry Spindelow	200	—	80
Bark Talbot	Henry Whyte	200	—	80
Virgin God Save Her	John Greynville	200	—	70
Spark	William Spark	200	—	80
Hope Hawkins of Plymouth	John Rivers	180	—	70
Bark Mannington	Ambrose Mannington	160	—	80

Orders of Battle

Name of Ship	Commander	Tons	Guns	Crew
Bark St Leger	John St Leger	160	—	80
Bark Bond	William Poole	150	—	70
Bark Bonner	Charles Caesar	150	—	70
Bark Hawkyns	William Snell	140	—	70
Elizabeth Founes	Roger Grant	100	—	60
Bear Yonge of London	John Yonge	140	—	70

Additions: 14 vessels under 100 tons

Narrow Seas Squadron (Lord Henry Seymour)

Queen's Ships (7)

Rainbow	Lord Henry Seymour	500	24	250
Vanguard	Sir William Wynter	500	42	250
Antelope	Sir Henry Palmer	400	24	170
Bull	Jeremy Turner	200	17	100
Tiger	John Bostocke	200	20	100
Tramontana	Luke Ward	150	21	80
Scout	Henry Ashley	100	18	80

Armed Merchant Vessels (7)

William of Ipswich	Barnaby Lowe	140	—	50
Katharine of Ipswich	Thomas Grymble	125	—	50
Primrose of Harwich	John Cardinal	120	—	40
Elizabeth of Dover	John Litgen	120	—	70
Grace of Yarmouth	William Musgrave	150	—	70
Mayflower of Lynn	Alexander Musgrave	150	—	70
William of Colchester	Thomas Lambert	140	—	50

Additions: 12 vessels under 100 tons

Reinforcements which joined Howard during the Campaign (6)

Sampson	John Wingfield	300	—	108
Frances of Fowey	John Rashley	140	—	60
Golden Ryall of Weymouth	—,120	—	50	
Samaritan of Dartmouth	—	250	—	100
William of Plymouth	—	120	—	60
Grace of Topsham	Walter Edney	100	—	50

Additions: 15 vessels under 90 tons

Armada 1588

Name of Ship	Commander	Tons	Guns	Crew
Armed Merchant Vessels sent from London to reinforce Seymour, 4 August (17)				
Susan Parnell of London	Nicholas Gorges	220	— ,80	
Violet of London	Martin Hawkins	220	—	60
Solomon of London	Edward Musgrave	170	—	80
Anne Francis of London	Charles Lister	180	—	70
George Bonaventure of London	Eleazar Hickman	200	—	80
Jane Bonaventure of London	Thomas Hallwood	100	—	80
Vineyard of London	Benjamin Cooke	160	—	60
George Noble of London	Richard Harper	120	14	60
Anthony of London	Richard Dove	100	12	50
Toby of London	Robert Cuttle	100	13	60
Salamander of Leigh	William Goodlad	110	12	55
Rose Lion of Leigh	Robert Duke	100	10	50
Antelope of London	Abraham Bonner	120	13	60
Jewel of Leigh	Henry Rawlyn	110	13	55
Pansy of London	William Butler	100	10	50
Prudence of Leigh	Richard Chester	120	12	60
Dolphin of Leigh	William Hare	110	11	55

Fifteen supply vessels, averaging 100 tons, were despatched from London to rendezvous with Howard off the Isle of Wight on 3 August.

Roll Call

Spanish

The following major ships are known to have been lost; in addition, a number of *pataches* and *zabras* were certainly casualties, but references to those 'missing' do not allow for the unknown number detached on specific missions, usually carrying orders and messages, that did not rejoin the Armada. Several, for example, probably remained in Flanders after being unable to rejoin the fleet before it was driven away at Gravelines. For that reason they are not included in the list below.

Squadron of Portugal
San Marcos, lost off Ireland
San Felipe, beached off Gravelines, captured by Dutch and sank
San Mateo, beached off Gravelines, captured by Dutch and sank

Squadron of Castile
San Juan, wrecked Stradleegh Sound, Ireland
La Trinidad, probably wrecked off Tralee, or foundered off Gravelines
San Juan Bautista, scuttled off Ireland

Squadron of Andalusia
Nuestra Señora del Rosario, captured, English Channel
Duquesna Santa Ana, wrecked Loughor Mor Bay, Co. Donegal, Ireland

Biscayan Squadron
Santa Ana, constructive loss, La Hogue France
El Gran Grin, wrecked off Clare Island, Ireland
La Concepción de Juanes del Cano, probably wrecked Co. Galway, Ireland
La Maria Juan, sunk off Gravelines

Armada 1588

Guipuzcoan Squadron
Santa Ana, blew up on return to Santander
Nuestra Señora del Rosa, wrecked Blasket Sound, Ireland
San Salvador, captured, English Channel
San Esteban, wrecked off Ireland

Levant Squadron
La Lavia, wrecked Streedagh Sound Co. Sligo, Ireland
La Rata Encoronada, wrecked Blacksod Bay, Ireland
San Juan de Sicilia, blown up (by English agent) Tobermory Bay, W. Scotland
La Trinidad Valencera, wrecked Glenagivney Bay, Ireland
La Anunciada, scuttled Shannon estuary, Ireland
San Nicholas Prodaneli, wrecked Co. Kerry, Ireland
La Juliana, wrecked off Donegal, Ireland
Santa Maria de Vison, wrecked off Co. Sligo, Ireland

Squadron of Hulks or Urcas
El Gran Grifon, wrecked off Fair Isle, Scotland
Castillo Negro, foundered north of Ireland
Barca de Amberg, foundered north of Ireland
San Pedro Mayor, wrecked Bigbury Bay N. Devon
San Pedro Meynor, missing, fate unknown
Falcon Blanco Mediano, wrecked off Ireland
Ciervo Volante, wrecked off Ireland
Santa Barbara, missing, fate unknown
Santiago, wrecked off Ireland

Galleasses of Naples
San Lorenzo, constructive loss after beaching at Calais
Girona, wrecked off Dunluce, N. Ireland

Galleys of Portugal
Diana, constructive loss after beaching near Bayonne

The Armada thus lost a total of thirty-six large vessels, though of these only six were as a direct consequence of enemy action. The human toll of the campaign is more difficult to calculate. The Battle of Gravelines cost the Spaniards an admitted 1,000 dead and 800 wounded, though all such casualty claims on both sides have to be assessed bearing in mind the common practice among contemporary commanders of understating their casualties, in order to carry on claiming dead men's pay.

Assuming the Gravelines total to be roughly correct, however, the Spaniards possibly lost at least another 1,000 men during the earlier Channel actions (including the 559-man crew of the *Nuestra Señora del Rosario*, captured by Drake).

Their greatest losses, however, were incurred in the shipwrecks on the Irish coast and the other sinkings that occurred during the voyage home. Again, exact figures are difficult to calculate, but the total complements of the ships known to have perished on the Irish coast or at sea were around 5,500 men. Perhaps 5,000 of these died. When the unknown – but certainly considerable – number of men who died later from wounds, disease, or starvation are added, it seems likely that at least 15,000 of the Armada's total complement of 29, 453 men died during or as a result of its ill-fated campaign.

The cost in senior officers was high. Of the squadron commanders, Hugo de Moncada of the galleasses of Naples was killed in action at Calais; Miguel de Oquendo died soon after returning to Corunna, probably from wounds suffered at Gravelines; the veteran, Juan Martinez de Recalde, who had been ill for much of the voyage, also died soon after reaching port. To King Philip, the most keenly felt personal loss was the dashing Don Alonso de Leiva, who was drowned in the wreck of the galleass, *Girona*.

English

Not a single English vessel was lost during the campaign and dockyard surveys made immediately afterwards suggest that even those ships constantly in the thick of the fighting, such as Howard's *Ark Royal* and Drake's *Revenge*, suffered no major structural damage.

English casualties in the fighting were claimed to have been no more than 100, and even bearing in mind the reservations stated above, it is clear they were comparatively light. The main losses came later, through starvation, sickness, and callous government neglect. Nobody troubled to record them at the time, so we can only estimate that perhaps half of the 16,000 men who served with the English fleet were dead by the end of the year: as great a proportion as those who died in the Armada.

Campaign Glossary

Almirante	A ship that carried the vice admiral of a Spanish squadron.
Arquebus	A predecessor of the musket, the arquebus differed in being shorter and firing a lighter bullet.
Bark or Barque	A small sailing ship with her rear mast rigged fore and aft, and the remaining two square-rigged.
Bow Chaser	A gun mounted in the bow of a ship, often used in pursuit in an attempt to cripple the quarry.
Cagework	The decoration on the hull of a ship.
Caliver	A firearm similar to the arquebus, but which, unlike the latter, fired a shot of standardised weight. Lighter and easier to manage than the matchlock musket, which had to be fired from a rest.
Capitana	Flagship of a Spanish fleet or squadron.
Carrack	First appearing in the early sixteenth century, these were three- or four-masted square-rigged ships, intended as merchant ships that were also capable of use in battle: they could be recognised by their characteristically high fore and stern superstructures.
Caravel	A three-masted lateen-rigged sailing vessel of 80–130 tons, noted for its speed, and usually lightly armed.
Careen	To swerve about, or tilt a ship on one side for cleaning or repair.
Close-hauled	A ship sailing with its sails hauled aft in order to sail as close as possible to the wind.
Coursing	Hunting or harrying: used by John Hawkins to describe English strategy against the Armada.
Crompster or Cromster	A shallow-drafted ship of about 200 tons, powerfully armed with a dozen or culverins and demi-culverins, widely used by the Dutch.

Culverin	An English gun, normally firing shot of between 10 and 18 pounds in weight. The equivalent Spanish piece was known as a *medio canone*.
Divers	Specially trained personnel used to repair underwater damage to ships. Some dived for brief periods without equipment. Others, probably including those used by Medina Sidonia, had all-leather suits, into which air was pumped from above using manual air pumps.
Downs, The	Large natural anchorage off the English coast between Dover and Margate.
Escorial	The combined monastery, palace, and fortress in the mountains north of Madrid: construction work commenced in 1567, and the Escorial became Philip II's favourite residence.
Fathom	Measurement of depth of the sea. One fathom equals 6 feet or 1.82 metres.
Felucca	A light fast sailing ship, lateen rigged, used for scouting and carrying despatches.
Flota	Spanish for fleet, though more specifically applied to the great convoys that annually brought gold, silver, and other goods to Spain from her colonies in the New World.
Flyboat	A fast shallow-draft two-masted gunboat, usually of less than 140 tons.
Galleon	A ship-rigged three or four masted vessel, usually of 450–1,500 tons, capable of carrying heavy guns, galleons were the most manoeuvrable and seaworthy vessels in the opposing fleets, and as such, their most powerful warships.
Galley	A lateen-rigged shallow-draft vessel, also powered by oars, making it highly manoeuvrable, and capable of short bursts of high speed: its main armament was mounted at the prow of the galley and fired forward. Galleys were mainly employed in the Mediterranean and Baltic, and found difficulty in coping with the heavy seas of the Atlantic.
Grapnel	An implement with several hooks, which when attached to a rope and thrown, was used to entangle the rigging on an opposing ship, in order to make boarding possible.

Campaign Glossary

Hulk	A wide-bellied cargo ship, usually with three masts, each carrying a single sail.
Knot	A measure of a ship's speed. One knot equals one nautical mile.
League	A measure of distance which might vary, but was roughly equivalent to 3 miles.
Lee (Leeward)	The side of a ship or fleet away from the wind.
Line of Battle	A fighting formation in which the ships of a fleet form a straight line in a predetermined order: despite some claims to the contrary, it is unlikely that this formation was employed during the Armada Campaign.
Luffing	Altering the course of a ship to run more nearly to the wind.
Lunula	Crescent-like battle-formation adopted by the Armada during most of the campaign in the Channel.
Maestro de Campo	Spanish military rank, roughly equivalent to colonel.
Musket	Matchlock firearms up to 20 pounds in weight, which were fired from fork rests by means of a length of lighted match cord which ignited gunpowder in the firing pan which in turn ignited a powder charge: it fired a ball weighing 1½ ounces.
Nao	(See Carrack)
Patache	(See Pinnace)
Pilot	A deep sea navigator
Pinnace (Spanish *patache*)	A two or three masted vessel of up to 70 tons, sometimes powered by oars, and used for scouting and carrying despatches. In combat the Spanish *pataches* provided close protection for the hulks. The term *zabra'* was sometimes used interchangeably by the Spaniards, though in some cases it seems to have referred to a larger similarly rigged vessel of up to 180 tons.
Privateer	An armed ship belonging to a private individual holding a government commission or authorisation to make war on that country's enemies. In many cases their actions were effectively piracy.
Queen's Ships	The ships of the Navy Royal, maintained by the Crown.
Saker Shot	A shot of between 5 and 7 pounds in weight.
Sea Room	A sufficient area of sea for a ship to turn or

	manoeuvre.
Shallops	A light craft, propelled by oars and sails, used for carrying despatches.
Socorro	A tactical unit employed by the Armada: initially referring to a second line fighting formation in the *lunula*, in practice the term also seems to have been employed for the roving 'battle groups' instituted by Medina Sidonia.
Stay	A rope or cable helping to secure a mast in position.
Tercio	A Spanish military unit, normally of about 3,000 men.
Urca	(See Hulk)
Warp	To tow a ship with boats or to move it by hauling on cables made fast to the shore or to buoys or anchors.
Weather-Gauge	The windward position in relation to another ship or fleet.
Zabra	(See Pinnace)

Bibliography

A full bibliography of all the hundreds of books and articles that have been written dealing with various aspects of the Armada Campaign would fill a book in their own right. To add to the confusion, some earlier works describe theories or suppositions (particularly on matters such as ship design and ordnance) that have since been radically revised by later research. The titles listed here either contain essential source material, the latest accepted research, or provide a reliable guide to the campaign as a whole. Most contain bibliographies to guide the interested reader still deeper into the story of the Armada.

Particularly recommended are Martin and Parker's book, *The Spanish Armada*, which provides a detailed overview of the entire campaign, and discusses the various contentious issues surrounding it, and the various titles by Angus Konstam. John Guilmartin's *Galleons and Galleys* is an excellent survey of the development and design of the ships which fought in the Armada Campaign.

Adams, Simon, *The Battle That Never Was: the Downs and the Armada Campaign*, in M. J. Rodriguez-Salgado and S. Adams (ed.), *England, Spain and the Gran Armada, 1585-89: Essays from the Anglo-Spanish Conferences, London and Madrid, 1988*, Edinburgh 1991

Cruickshank, G., *Elizabeth's Army*, Oxford 1966

Fernandez-Armesto, Felipe, *The Spanish Armada: the Experience of War in 1588*, Oxford 1988

Flanaghan, Laurence, *Irish Wrecks of the Spanish Armada*, Dublin 1995

Gallagher, P. and D. W. Cruickshank (eds), *God's Obvious Design: Papers for the Spanish Armada Symposium, Sligo, 1988*, London 1990

Guilmartin, John, *Galleons and Galleys*, London 2002

Hanson, Neil, *The Confident Hope of a Miracle: the True History of the Spanish Armada*, London 2003

Howarth, David, *The Voyage of the Armada: the Spanish Story*, London 2001

Aftermath

Hume, Martin Andrew Sharp (ed.), *Calendar of State Papers Relating to English Affairs preserved in or originally belonging to the Archives of Simancas, vol.4,* London 1899

Konstam, R. Angus, *The Armada Campaign 1588,* Oxford 2001

Konstam, R. Angus, *Elizabethan Sea Dogs,* Oxford 2002

Konstam, R. Angus, *Renaissance War Galley,* Oxford 2003

Konstam, R. Angus, *Spanish Galleon,* Oxford 2004

Laughton, Sir John Knox (ed), *State Papers Relating to the Defeat of the Spanish Armada,* reprinted Aldershot 1987

McKee, Alexander, *From Merciless Invaders: The Defeat of the Spanish Armada,* London 1988

Martin, C.J., *Full Fathom Five: Wrecks of the Spanish Armada,* London 1975

Martin, Colin J.M. and Parker, Geoffrey, *The Spanish Armada,* London 1988

Mattingly, Garrett, *The Defeat of the Spanish Armada,* London 1959

Parker, Geoffrey, *The Army of Flanders and the Spanish Road, 1567-1659: The Logistics of Spanish Victory and Defeat in the Low Countries' Wars,* Cambridge 1976

Parker, Geoffrey, *The Grand Strategy of Philip II,* London 1998

Pierson, Peter, *Commander of the Armada: The Seventh Duke of Medina Sidonia,* Yale 1989

Roberts, Keith, *Matchlock Musketeer, 1588–1688,* Oxford 2002

Rodger, N.A.M., *The Safeguard of the Sea: A Naval History of Britain, I: 1660–1649,* London 1997

Rodriguez-Salgado, Mia J., *et al, Armada 1588–1988: An International Exhibition to Commemorate the Spanish Armada,* London 1988

Stenuit, Robert, *Treasures of the Armada,* Newton Abbot 1972

Thomas, David A., *The Illustrated Armada Handbook,* London 1988

Tincey, John, *The Spanish Armada,* Oxford 2000

Usherwood, Stephen (ed), *The Great Enterprise: The History of the Spanish Armada as Revealed in Contemporary Documents,* London 1982

Walker, Bryce S., *The Armada,* New York 1981

Index

Index

Index

Index